Other Books by Crystal Springs Books

MAKING THE CONNECTION
Learning Skills Through Literature
by Patricia Pavelka

MAKING THE CONNECTION
Learning Skills Through Literature (3-6)
by Patricia Pavelka

I CAN LEARN!
Strategies and Activities
for Gray-Area Children
by Gretchen Goodman

INCLUSIVE CLASSROOMS
FROM A TO Z
by Gretchen Goodman

OUR BEST ADVICE
The Multiage Problem Solving Handbook
by Jim Grant, Bob Johnson, and Irv Richardson

THE MULTIAGE HANDBOOK
A Comprehensive Resource
for Multiage Practices
Compiled by Jim Grant and Irv Richardson

MULTIAGE Q&A
101 Practical Answers
to Your Most Pressing Questions
Written and Compiled by
Jim Grant, Bob Johnson, and Irv Richardson

THE LOOPING HANDBOOK
Teachers and Students
Progressing Together
Written by
Jim Grant, Bob Johnson, and Irv Richardson

CREATING & MANAGING
Learning Centers
A THEMATIC APPROACH

CREATING & MANAGING
Learning Centers

A THEMATIC APPROACH

by Phoebe Bell Ingraham

Crystal Springs Books • Peterborough, New Hampshire

Printed in the United States of America
01 00 99 98 97 96 6 5 4 3 2 1

Published and distributed by:

Crystal Springs Books
Ten Sharon Road, Box 500
Peterborough, NH 03458-0500
1-800-321-0401

Cataloging-in-Publication Data

Ingraham, Phoebe Bell, 1951 -
      Creating and managing learning centers : a thematic approach /
Phoebe Bell Ingraham.—1st ed.
[192] p. : cm.
Includes bibliographies.
Summary : This title shows how to create learning centers tied to
curriculum requirements, how to teach children to work in learning
centers, and what learning centers to include in the classroom, with
examples and activities.

ISBN 1-884548-06-7
1. Classroom learning centers 2. Teaching. 3. Learning. I. Title.
371.302   '82— dc 20   1997   CIP
LC Card Number : 96-83280

Editor-in-Chief: Aldene Fredenburg
Contributing Editor: Deborah Sumner

Cover and Book Design: Susan Dunholter
Photos: Tim Reeder, Reeder Photography

The artwork on the center charts on pages 44, 45, and 50, and on the
reproducibles on pages 165 and 167-170, is used with the permission
of Highlights For Children.

This book is dedicated to my mother,

Cynthia K. Bell

whose love of learning and desire to write
inspired me; and my father,

Richard H. Bell

whose wisdom and constant support
have guided me through life.
I am truly blessed to have had such
loving and gifted parents.

◉ ACKNOWLEDGMENTS ◉

Thank you to all those who supported my efforts in writing this book. It could not have been possible without your friendship, patience and assistance:

My husband Ted, for his support and confidence in me, and for his computer instruction.

Our children, Stacy, Beth, and Brad, for the understanding, encouragement, and pride in me they provided as this book was written and rewritten.

Gretchen, Rick, Susan, and Betsy, who were, and are, the very best of role models a little sister ever had to live up to.

My editors, Aldene Fredenburg and Deborah Sumner, whose advice meant so much to this book.

Jim Grant, Jay LaRoche, and Lorraine Walker, who never seemed to doubt that I could actually write this book.

The teachers and friends I had to leave but never can forget: Judith Penry, Nancy Drummond, Lisa Churchey, Betsy Patrick, Marge Sumner, and Bonnie Williams. Mr. Ison is right. To be a great teacher, you must first be a great person. You are all the very best.

The teachers and friends who read and reread and criticized with kindness and great expertise: Carla Amburgey, Linda See, Susan Voyles, and Bevin Gumm.

My patient photographer, Tim Reeder.

Mr. Phil Fox, Principal and Director of Special Programs, Lockland City Schools; Meredith Fritsch, Secretary and Creative Director, Arlington Primary School.

All my kindergartners, past and present, who have so patiently taught me how much they love to learn, and how they do it best. As Clifford says with such assurance, "I can do it!"

And to Nancy, who never lost sight of what it's all about. Your spirit lives on in the pages of this book. I miss you, Nance.

◙ CONTENTS ◙

Introduction

We teach a subject not to produce little living libraries on that subject, but rather to get a student to think mathematically for himself, to consider matters as an historian does, to take part in the process of knowledge-getting. Knowing is a process, not a product.

— Jerome Bruner,
*Toward a Theory
of Instruction*

 t is an exciting time to be a teacher. A multitude of changes are taking place in classrooms today; teachers are being given more responsibility for what goes on in their classrooms, and they are learning how to pass this responsibility on to their students.

Reading and writing are a part of learning in every area of the curriculum, because that's the way it is in the real world, and that's the way we learn. Real books are being used in reading. Children write in today's classrooms out of a real need to communicate their thoughts and ideas with others.

Lessons about science are occurring outside the classroom, as children interact with the real world—their world. Math concepts are tried and tested out of a real need to understand how and why things occur. Children are learning that they are part of a global community, and that they can act as individuals to make a difference in that community.

All these lessons are intertwined to give meaning and continuity for the child. And when it's time to determine how well the lessons have been learned, children are allowed to demonstrate their ability to utilize processes and specific information, rather than by taking standardized tests, to discover what it is they do not know. Children are learning to *love learning*; they are learning *how to learn*; they are learning that they are *capable of learning* whatever interests them.

I have used centers in my classrooms in some form since my first year of teaching. I've probably made every mistake possible, and spent countless hours adapting what I do. I've changed room plans, changed lesson plan formats, changed classrooms, changed buildings, changed grade levels, and changed thematic units. I could probably run my centers in my sleep. I thought this book would write itself. It didn't.

This book was first inspired by the many teachers who visited my classrooms and told me how much they enjoyed watching my students learn. They told me this is the way they want to teach! Then they asked me how to do it. They thought the answer was an easy one.

When Jim Grant of The Society For Developmental Education advised me to write down my workshop into a book, he assured me that I could do it. He even promised to publish it. That was an offer too good to refuse, especially when I was convinced the book would write itself!

I began writing the book as teachers from across the country attended my presentations and thanked me, saying, "That was just what I needed to hear!" They helped me see what to include and how to describe the process I go through in my classroom that makes my centers work for my students. Their encouragement made it seem so easy.

I completed the book as I watched my student teachers gradually take over supervision of center time. No matter how hard they worked, sometimes things fell apart. As I analyzed why things weren't functioning for them as they did for me, I came to understand the subtle differences that can make or break quality learning experiences. Becoming an observer made writing this easier.

And finally, I edited the book again and again (and again!) as I thought of the courageous teachers who have called me from across town and across the country, struggling to change their classrooms into child-centered environments. They were good teachers who needed some support and affirmation as they gave up old habits in order to share the learning process with their students. I heard in their voices how very difficult it was, and felt that I owed it to them to offer some ideas that have worked for me. They gave me the courage to take the risk and keep writing.

To all of those educators who have inspired and coerced me to complete this book, thank you! I hope it brings me into your classrooms, and answers those questions you didn't think to ask when we were together.

Have a great school year watching your students enjoy the learning process!

Planning and Creating Centers

he first part of *Creating and Managing Learning Centers: A Thematic Approach* gives you background information that will allow you to feel comfortable about using learning centers in your classroom.

In *Chapter 1*, I explain different types of centers. I show you what centers offer for your students, and how they can change your room into an active, child-centered classroom.

Chapter 2 helps you begin to make the physical changes in your classroom necessary in order to utilize learning centers in your daily routine. I offer ideas on how to plan your environment to allow your students to become active participants in their learning, while allowing you to maintain control as the teacher. I also discuss how to relate learning centers to your curricular objectives.

Classrooms that encourage students to take more control in their learning must have specific strategies for maintaining organization. In this type of structure, the teacher's role changes as students are taught how to learn rather than what to learn. *Chapter 3* contains critical information about teaching your students how to work in learning centers, as well as advice on how to create an active yet productive environment.

Planning for the year is as important in this type of structure as in any classroom, but you must find ways to involve your students in the process. This is often a difficult aspect of center-oriented environments for many teachers. It isn't difficult to come up with fun activities to place into centers, but how do you utilize center activities to teach your curricular objectives? *Chapter 4* explains how the teacher can take student interests into consideration without giving up control of the curriculum. This chapter also gives ideas for integrating your curriculum to ensure that meaningful connections can be made by your students to allow them to utilize specific skills and concrete facts.

It is impossible to ignore the role evaluation takes in the active classroom. *Chapter 5* discusses authentic assessment strategies to use to help you maintain student progress. Authentic assessment strategies are both descriptive and prescriptive, so that teaching, learning, and evaluation become parts of a cycle in each child's successful development. I have included many resources to help you locate alternative assessments for your students.

Part 1 is designed to help you know where to begin to make changes in your teaching. You will find answers to many questions you may have about teaching thematically and involving students in experiential learning opportunities. This portion of the book gives you the background you need in order to maintain a child-centered classroom with success and assurance.

Chapter 1

What Are Centers?

A good school asks much of its students all the time, makes them do the work if they can, gets them into the habit of taking responsibility for their lives. In so doing it expresses respect for them, a respect that can elicit responsibility.

— Theodore R. Sizer,
*Horace's School: Redesigning
the American High School*

earning centers are self-descriptive. Physically, centers are simply small areas of a classroom set aside for learning to take place. They might be called stations, laboratories (labs), or learning areas. Their unique contribution comes from the type of activities or specific tasks they offer in order to enable children's knowledge to develop.

• The activities are meaningful for the children, relating to concepts they have learned during total class lessons.

• They arise out of a child's need to know or do. For example, when learning about primary and secondary colors, children have the opportunity, in a learning center activity, to mix the colors, discovering for themselves that every time you mix red and yellow, you get shades of orange.

• Children have a purpose, or intrinsic motivation, for completing the activities. The tasks involve the children in processes that confirm or deny information they have been discussing as a class. Intrinsic motivation occurs when a child wants to complete work because of a real need to accomplish the task, such as writing a note to a friend or writing in a journal to express thoughts or feelings.

• The desire to complete activities often comes from lessons taught by the teacher. For example, after a lesson on magnetism, young children work in the science center with a variety of magnets (bar, horseshoe, magnets of different strengths, etc.), playing with magnetic marbles, predicting and sorting magnetic and non-magnetic materials. In this way, children can investigate for themselves the information they learn through their total group lessons and through their reading.

• Centers have a variety of developmentally appropriate activities from which each child may choose. The projects vary in ability level, so that every child in the class is able to complete some tasks with success, but each child is also encouraged to extend his learning and try something more challenging.

Developmentally appropriate instructional practices include two dimensions: age appropriateness and individual appropriateness.

First, the environment must be age-appropriate, containing activities and materials that are most suited to children of the age range of the students in your class. The curricular objectives assigned to each grade level by your school district can be your guide here. Every child in the class should be exposed to lessons and activities that teach the objectives appropriate and deemed necessary for students at this level. (This assumes that your curriculum is well-written, with sound knowledge of child development.) The learning tasks chosen for each center should include tasks that facilitate the learning of these concepts and skills.

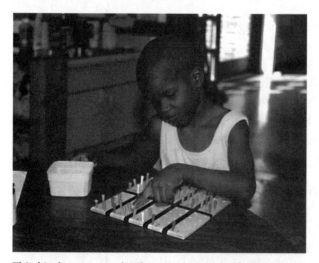

This kindergartner checks over his work after completing a counting activity in the math center.

Second, the environment should be individually appropriate, or child-specific, in order to meet the needs of each child. Every classroom contains children of varying ages and developmental stages. Every classroom is filled with diverse individuals coming to school with a wide span of experiences and educational support. Whether you have a classroom that is labeled with a specific grade, a multiage grouping, or an inclusive classroom, you must consider each child's level of maturity, experience, prior knowledge, and ability to learn.

When you teach to your students on an individual basis, you have a multiage philosophy. Offering tasks at a variety of levels in each center will enable every child in your class to meet with success at certain activities, while challenging her in creative ways. This does not occur in the first week, but it should be a goal of your program.

The Child-Centered Classroom

Providing a center-oriented classroom takes more than rearranging the furniture. The teacher must be secure in his knowledge of child development and curriculum objectives, and feel comfortable with classroom management strategies that work for him. Children will be given choice with responsibility, and the teacher must feel confident in his ability to know what each child is working on, why she is choosing to spend her time on that work, and how to redirect her activity if and when it is necessary to step in.

The teacher must be willing to share the responsibility for managing the environment with the children, and feel comfortable with his ability to teach them how to handle this responsibility; otherwise, they will be constantly off-task, keeping themselves busy on inappropriate activities rather than accomplishing tasks for learning.

The center environment allows for cooperation among children who use oral and written language to confirm or reject hypotheses. Tasks that encourage thinking and reasoning skills are utilized and the classroom structured to foster decision-making skills, independence, and self-sufficiency. The activities placed in the centers encourage creativity, problem solving, critical thinking, and concrete learning with manipulatives.

Some activities should require children to think abstractly and transfer what they learn from their manipulative tasks to a higher level. Tasks should be varied, some designed to be completed independently, while others necessitate small group cooperation.

Many activities are based on a central theme that is woven throughout all the learning centers in the room. In this way, children will be able to make the necessary connections to pull information from their memory to use in solving new problems.

Designing your day around centers does not mean that your children simply take their workbooks and ditto sheets off to small group areas to complete them as they choose. Nor does it mean that children are simply free to choose whatever activity they please, and if they wish to change work in the middle of a project, they may. Structure and direction must be built into the environment if children are expected to work within it.

Running a classroom organized around centers means that the teacher will be actively involved with the learning process throughout the day, moving from one area to another, working with individuals and small groups. The day goes by quickly, for the teacher rarely has an opportunity to sit down. Everyone is busy all the time.

Providing the Structure

In order to understand how to create the child-centered classroom without giving in to complete anarchy, it might help to think of an analogy. Consider the traditional classroom as a crustacean, with its skeletal system (exoskeleton) on the outside of its body. It is kept intact, or maintained, externally. The structure is imposed upon it, leaving little opportunity for individuality or diversity to grow. Inside, its muscles move about, but are always confined and controlled by the rigid exoskeleton.

Now picture the human body. The skeletal system gives support from within, allowing more freedom of movement, more creative development, from the muscular structure of the individual. This is how my classroom operates; I am the skeletal system, giving support and direction from within. The individual students and their actions add to the environment, making adaptations as needed.

Each year, my classroom varies (just as human bodies do), as something is added to or deleted from the structure. The individuals are allowed to reshape the environment of my classroom so that it meets their needs and matches their specific learning styles. My structure is still there, giving support and stability, but the activity of the classroom is constantly modified to accommodate the personality of the new community.

The teacher who controls from the exterior must keep all the interior movement organized. But the teacher who manages from within gives a foundational structure, allowing individuals to branch out and develop in unique ways. The structure is definitely still present, but it is not always visible to the casual observer. This is partly because children are given more responsibility in a child-centered classroom.

Observers see young children making decisions and controlling their activity, and some assume that the teacher has completely

Creating an environment where children take on much of the responsibility for their learning actually frees me to give more individual support and attention to each child.

given up these responsibilities. This is not true; the teacher respects the children's ability to make decisions and take responsibility for their learning, but she carefully instructs them in how to learn, how to make wise decisions in the classroom, and how to complete necessary tasks. The child-centered teacher continues to give support and advice as it is required, carefully guiding each child through

(continued on page 20)

ARLINGTON PRIMARY KINDERGARTEN
Mrs. Phoebe Ingraham

WELCOME TO CENTER TIME!

You'll be hearing about center time all year. This is our independent work time, when the children choose the work station, or center, that they will go to. Your child should visit one to three centers per day. Centers your child consistently chooses on Monday are very likely his favorites, while those chosen consistently on Friday are usually more difficult or least enjoyed by him. I encourage the children to work in every center each week, but I do allow repetition. Sometimes new tasks are introduced in a center in the middle of the week, after your child has worked there. Other times, your child might be working on a project that is taking additional time and care. I respect his need to spend additional time in a center.

Most centers have a variety of tasks that your child will choose from. Often, centers will have both a selection of activities and a specific task that is mandatory.

If your child repeatedly tells you that he didn't do anything at school, it might be helpful to ask him what centers he went to. This paper will help you understand what each center emphasizes, and why it is so important to our curriculum. You may want to keep it in a safe place so that you can refer to it throughout the year.

Art Tables and the Easel

Art simultaneously develops all areas of a child: fine motor, large motor, emotional, cognitive, symbolic communication, and social skills. Math skills such as how to use space, thick and thin, etc., are learned as we complete art jobs. One table is used to complete specific projects, following directions. The other table is used for creative art experiences. At the easel, a child may develop his muscle systems by using his whole body to make large strokes.

Role Play

The most productive learning experiences come from children's natural play. Our role play area is related to our thematic units in science and social studies. It is sometimes a house, a pet store, or a doctor's office. Such important concepts as self-worth, cooperation, self-control, and imagination are nurtured in our role play center. The children will use writing and reading for real purposes in their dramatic play. This will encourage literacy development, as they are motivated to use these skills to accomplish tasks that have meaning and a purpose for them.

Blocks

Our large muscle area holds much more than just blocks, but that is what we call it most of the time. Block building is science: gravity, stability, weight, trial and error, inductive reasoning, and interaction of forces. It is math: classification, measurement, volume, area, sequence, number, fractions, height and weight, depth and length. Block building is physical development: eye-hand coordination, visual perception, hand manipulation, balancing. It is also art, social studies, language, and social skills. Our block center is an important area, to girls as well as boys.

I send this letter home to parents each year to explain the importance of center time and what parents may expect their children to accomplish in each center. (It might be wise to create a letter for boys and one for girls to solve the "he/she" dilemma when communicating to parents about their children.)

Games

The selection of activities in this center changes regularly, but the concepts being taught remain the same. Math- , language- , and science-oriented games build cognitive development. Small muscle control, eye-hand coordination, and visual discrimination are developed with puzzles, stencils, and other manipulatives. Social and emotional skills are also developed in the games center, as the children learn to share, take turns, and follow rules of different games.

Language, Writing, Journals, and Library

These centers house the activities your child will use to build his literacy skills this year. The language center deals mostly with the alphabet, and how letters make words we can read and write. The writing center is our space to practice the mechanics of handwriting, as well as learning how to use written language creatively. We will be writing in our journals regularly, but the journal center will be available for extra practice or conferencing with the teacher. Our library is filled with favorite books, flannel board stories, books on the tape recorder, and puppets. Many of the books are ones I read aloud, repeating them often to teach specific literacy skills.

Math

Our math center gives children many opportunities to manipulate tangible objects. They will classify objects, discovering relationships between them, form sets, make patterns, and seriate according to size. Because math for a young child should be a concrete activity rather than an abstract concept, few papers will come home. Our math center is one area where we develop the awareness that we can solve problems and create solutions.

Science

Curiosity, experimentation, discovery, observation, decision making, and problem solving are all important abilities we nurture in our science center. Math and scientific concepts such as classification, comparison, and sequencing are reinforced. We learn to draw conclusions. We learn to be scientists as we go about our lives on this lovely planet, Earth. Specific units include transportation, colors, dinosaurs, nutrition, weather, magnetism, our five senses, living things, and space, as well as others the children wish to investigate.

Geography

Geography is a fascinating area of study that really excites young learners. We will begin the year with a general study of physical geography on earth. After this, we'll learn about a different continent each month. So much is developed in this center: map skills, fine motor development, eye-hand coordination, multi-cultural literature, respect for others, music, communication and language, the environment, as well as an awareness of how connected all people are on this planet.

Computer Lab

Your child will have the opportunity to visit the computer lab during center time. He may work on writing, math, science, or art activities, or play computer games based on a current thematic unit, while learning valuable computer skills.

the learning process, while providing the scaffolding, or foundation, that is needed to understand new information.

Sharing responsibility with young children is often difficult for teachers, for we have not been taught this skill. We don't always know how to teach children how to learn. We get lots of instruction in how to teach math and grammar, but few lessons in how to teach Christopher, Emily, Dominique, and Bridgette.

Creating the Environment

First, you must create an environment that will allow students to work independently. Learning centers must be planned and arranged in your classroom; each center must have learning tools available to the children. Books, dictionaries, paper, computers, paint, staplers, tape, manipulatives, blank books, tape recorders, and markers — all the supplies that they need to complete a task — must be available to them.

The children must be taught how to use and care for these materials, just as they must be taught how to complete each task and manage their work. And they must feel a sense of pride about and ownership of their classroom, and take part in its responsibilities; this is essential in operating a child-centered environment.

You should plan the centers for your classroom well in advance of the children's arrival

Putting on a puppet show. The puppet stage, a temporary center created from a box covered in paper, could also be placed in the role play area or the library as a permanent activity.

at school. Different types of centers can be arranged in any classroom. Basically, they fall into two categories: temporary and permanent.

Temporary Centers

Temporary centers are areas of your classroom set up as learning stations for a specific activity. Each station will change completely as your thematic unit changes.

For example, in the fall, a "Fabulous Friends" center might be set up during a unit on friendship. Each child is invited to bring a small display of items important to her, that tell a little about herself (for instance, a collection, family pictures, a baby toy, and something she made herself). As students visit the center, they look at each child's things and learn more about each other. When the friendship unit is over, the friends center disappears, another center containing activities based on the next thematic unit taking its place.

Temporary centers can also be arranged around a classroom set up in a more traditional manner. While the majority of the day is spent at desks in one area of the room, a block of time is set aside for center activities. This is a good way for a teacher to make the transition into center-type activities. The children are allowed to choose which center to visit, though they need to complete a specified list of tasks within a given amount of time.

The teacher might also choose to control the groupings. For example, five centers can be set up during a thematic unit on dinosaurs (see Fig. 1-1, page 21). These can include:

- a math activity, such as creating patterns with dinosaurs

- a mural, diorama, triarama, or other art-oriented project

- a specific science project, such as a model of a dinosaur skeleton

- a cooperative food project, such as making "dinosaur" (deviled) eggs

- a table for small group instruction with the teacher; this can involve specific math concepts taught through the dinosaur theme, or a writing project introducing report writing

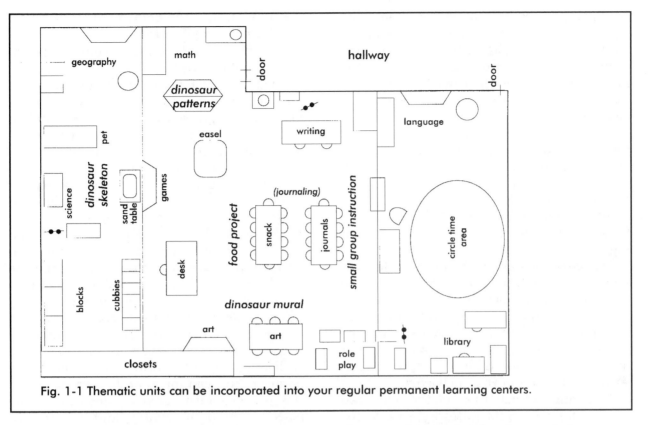

Fig. 1-1 Thematic units can be incorporated into your regular permanent learning centers.

In this setup, the class can be divided into five groups that remain intact until all children have completed every center. Groups of this nature are flexible, made for a one-week period while the class works at these tasks. Children can be grouped heterogeneously one week, according to instructional needs another week (for instance, a teacher may group children needing similar mini-lessons together), and to work cooperatively on a project another week. Decisions specific to the structure of the classroom are made by the teacher according to the thematic unit, students' needs, and the specific objectives for that week.

On Monday, students are assigned a center. Children work with the members of their center group, completing the task at just that center for the day. Each day, the groups rotate until, by the end of the week, every group has completed the work at each center. (This can also be done with four groups and four specific tasks, leaving Friday open to bring the total class together for a common sharing time about the thematic unit.)

This setup requires careful planning of specific activities, for each activity must take the groups an equal amount of time. While it's somewhat easier for the teacher to manage, it doesn't allow for student choice in task completion or give as much flexibility in planning for individualization.

While many teachers begin utilizing centers in this way, it's only a beginning. An important element of a truly child-centered classroom involves the child in the ownership of the learning process. Self-discipline, self-reliance, and self-direction are taught only when the child is allowed to take responsibility for herself. If the teacher is always in complete control of the groupings and how the tasks are completed, the children never begin to manage their own learning.

In a truly child-centered environment, teachers must include learning experiences in task completion, decision making, and working cooperatively with others. To provide this, a teacher must make the decision to set up permanent centers and give more responsibility to the children.

Permanent Centers

Permanent centers are fixed areas of your classroom designed around the content areas in your curriculum. They remain, for the most part, permanent areas throughout the year.

In this structure, the entire classroom is designed around curricular centers; children work in areas such as math, science, reading or library, writing, and dramatic play. As thematic units change, the centers remain, but many specific jobs within each center will change.

Some of the materials housed in each center remain there for the entire year. They are generic manipulatives that can be used to teach a variety of specific skills within that curricular area. Examples of these within a math center include Unifix™ cubes, Cuisinaire™ rods, attribute blocks, and counting beads.

However, it's also important to add other tasks, planned specifically around each thematic unit. These activities stay in the center for a short period of time, allowing you to integrate the curriculum. In this way, the specific objectives in each subject area are taught in a holistic framework, linking specific tasks with real-life use of the knowledge.

Examples of activities for the math center that fall within this category, specific to a unit on Ocean Life, might include:

- seashells for weighing, patterning, and counting
- jars with different amounts of sand for practice in seriation
- a jar of shells for estimating total number
- a variety of fish for sorting and classifying

All materials in both categories, generic and theme-specific, are maintained in the math center simultaneously.

The use of the generic materials is taught at the beginning of the school year. The materials and activities specific to thematic units are introduced during each new unit, and simply added to the generic materials. When children have completed tasks specific to the thematic unit, they will then be able to repeat activities with the generic materials, reinforcing concepts learned previously and connecting them to the information they are learning within the framework of the current thematic unit.

A Combination of Permanent and Temporary Centers

Another way to arrange your classroom into center areas is to utilize both permanent, curricular center areas and temporary centers. For example, your room may contain permanent library, writing, math, and building block areas. Additionally, temporary centers are placed in the classroom housing activities specific to each thematic unit. Often in this type of arrangement, there is space for one to three temporary centers, all related in some way to the thematic unit.

For example, during a unit on health and nutrition, the literacy, math, and writing centers can all have activities that incorporate the thematic unit. A grocery store can also be set up in the classroom for dramatic play. Science-oriented activities promoting health and good foods can be organized in another center, which can also include an art activity, such as a collage of favorite foods. A third temporary center can incorporate cooking activities using healthy snacks. Recipes can be placed around the center, and children allowed to recreate such snacks as peanut butter crackers or fruit salad. Children can also be encouraged to create their own recipes, writing down the ingredients and steps in preparation, and trying it out themselves.

Resources

Beckman, Carol; Simmons, Roberta; and Thomas, Nancy. *Channels to Children*. Colorado Springs: Channels to Children, 1982.

Bredekamp, Sue (Ed.). *Developmentally Appropriate Practice in Early Childhood Programs Serving Children From Birth Through Age 8*. Washington, D.C.: National Association for the Education of Young Children, 1987.

Croft, Doreen J., and Hess, Robert D. *An Activities Handbook for Teachers of Young Children*. Boston: Houghton Mifflin, 1975.

Northeast Foundation for Children. *A Notebook for Teachers: Making Changes in the Elementary Curriculum*. Greenfield, MA: Northeast Foundation for Children, 1993.

Wood, Chip. *Yardsticks*. Greenfield, MA: Northeast Foundation for Children, 1994.

Chapter 2

Creating Your Physical Environment

For the past two centuries or so, we have come to believe that what children need to know in order to become happy and productive adults can be learned by sitting in a crowded room and listening to an adult talk in an abstract language, while surrounded by other immature children. It takes a gigantic act of faith to believe that this is possible, but we seem increasingly willing to delude ourselves on this account, despite all evidence to the contrary.

— Mihaly Csikszentmihalyi, "Contexts of Optimal Growth in Childhood," from *Daedalus*, Winter 1993

 he first stage in creating a child-centered classroom is to plan the physical environment. Choosing the centers you wish to incorporate into your plan, then designing a floor plan that meets all the needs of your situation, is both creative and exhausting.

It is helpful to try this step with another teacher. Often, we get stuck in old habits, leaving furniture and centers in their place simply because that's where they've always been. Another person helps in this stage of planning, offering a new perspective and fresh ideas.

Keep in mind that you do not need to remove all desks from your room, and you do not need to purchase all new furniture. In order to know what you need to remove, and what you may need to add, you first need to decide how you want your classroom to look.

Step One: Start With a Plan

First, decide what centers you wish to have in your classroom. I plan my year thematically, fitting the instruction of specific skills required by my school district into interdisciplinary units. This approach encourages the integration of curricular areas like math, science, and geography in order to teach a broad concept.

The curricular nature of my thematic planning directs my classroom environment: I teach a concept through experiences in these curricular divisions, so my classroom should be divided into these same areas. Reading and writing are utilized in every curricular area to encourage an understanding and a thoughtful application of these general concepts.

It may be easiest to begin with general areas, and become more specific as you gain experience in this approach. For example, divide your space into literacy development centers, cognitive development centers, creative development centers, physical development centers, and social and emotional centers (see Fig. 2-1).

It is important to note that every center in my classroom nurtures all of these developmental areas in some way, but I emphasize a particular domain when I place an activity into a center.

For example, while I include literacy interactions in every center of my classroom—children have opportunities to read and write while building with blocks, investigating a fossil, creating a work of art with paints, experiencing another culture, making an ABC pattern, and operating a grocery store — writing is such an important part of my students' total development that I have several centers designed specifically to encourage a variety of elements in writing:

• I want my children to take the time and effort to write creatively on a regular basis, so there is a specific center set aside for that task.

• I believe that legible handwriting is a skill that must be taught and practiced, but it must be connected to real-life activities in order for it to be utilized; so I incorporate handwriting activities into my creative writing center.

• My journal center involves the children in reflection and in recording their personal thoughts.

• I want my students to feel confident as readers and writers, and to do this, they must become fluent at these tasks. This takes practice in specific skills inherent in these activities. Therefore, I set up a language center for practicing specific reading, writing, and spelling strategies, as well as a library to encourage them to spend time reading.

Similarly, I design activities specifically to promote social and emotional development in the games, role play, and dramatic play areas, even though social and emotional development is nurtured in every center. And while math principles are used throughout our day and in many of our centers (blocks, cooking, science, geography, library, art, writing, and games), we set aside activities and spend time concentrating on the acquisition of specific skills within our curriculum in the math center.

Look at your classroom. Depending upon the size of the room and the number of students you have in your class, try dividing your room into the above five categories. Think about the needs each area will require. For example:

• Literacy centers will need plenty of light and electrical outlets so children can listen to tapes of books or make tapes of themselves reading. Areas for children to write need table or desk space.

I like my literacy centers close to the door, so the children and visitors notice that, first and foremost, we *read and write*!

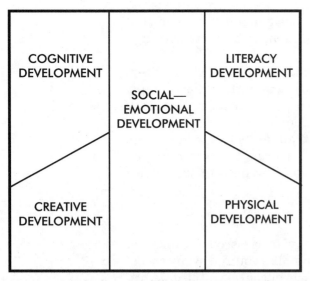

Fig. 2-1 Divide the available space into general areas for different types of centers.

• Cognitive centers also need electrical outlets, plus table space for students to work at writing tasks. There should be plenty of space for working with manipulatives in small groups, as well as for storing materials and a wide variety of resource books.

I like to incorporate a window near my science center, so the children will have opportunities to observe the world outside.

• Creative development centers should include space close to a sink and plenty of shelves to hold all the "junk" so necessary for creative projects. Plenty of table space is also important. If possible, it's nice to have two tables: one for teacher-directed activities and one for self-directed creations. In kindergarten and primary classrooms, an easel should be included.

• Physical development centers will need a lot of space, especially for kindergarten and primary classrooms. There should be room for a balance beam, bean bag toss, blocks, and large motor games. These activities will rotate through this area.

It is wise to place this center in a corner, away from traffic areas, and on a rug or carpeted area. It's best *not* to place your gross motor area against a thin wall, where another class might be disturbed by the noise of falling blocks.

For upper elementary children, fine motor development and eye-hand coordination need more attention than gross motor development. In these classrooms, it might be beneficial to incorporate the physical development centers into the social and emotional development centers. This will allow more space for the children to move within their groups. Manipulative games will encourage both areas of development simultaneously.

• Social and emotional development areas are more prevalent in kindergarten and primary classrooms than in upper elementary grades. As mentioned above, older elementary children participate in a variety of cooperative learning groups that nurture their social and emotional growth.

However, these areas are prime candidates for a temporary center in your class-room. Older children will benefit from occasional space to develop puppet shows, creative drama, and reader's theater. Allow ample opportunities for these experiences as your space allows.

Once you have established the general locations in your classroom for each grouping, you can divide them into specific centers that best meet the needs of your students and match your curriculum and the goals you have set for yourself and your students (Fig. 2-2):

• Math and science centers are the easiest centers for which to create experiential learning activities.

• Depending upon your writing program, you may wish to include an area for creative writing or journaling.

• Journals might be included within *each* center, particularly in late primary classrooms. For example, math journals might be included as an activity in the math center, while a round-robin journal could be kept on specific books of interest in your reading or library center.

A round-robin journal allows children to add their comments about a particular book or topic. Place a small journal in your read-

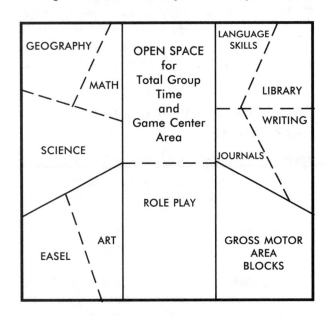

Fig. 2-2 Once you've divided your classroom into general areas, you can begin to place specific centers within each area.

ing or library center, and ask open-ended questions to start the conversation about the story. For example, in a journal for the book, *Stellaluna*, write the question:

"Have you ever done something that seemed normal for you, but attracted much attention from others? Why do you think that happened?"

Or you might simply ask, "Would you rather be a bird or a bat? Why?" Allow several children to react in writing before asking another question.

Journals designed for an author study might also be used in this manner. For example, during an author study of Mem Fox, place several of her books on a shelf, along with a "Mem Fox Books Journal." On the first page, list the books you've read together and have in your class library. Include blank pages for the children to write a response to their favorite Mem Fox book. When the author study is complete, this journal may be read aloud to compare and contrast the reading experiences and reflections that your students had when reading her books.

You do not need to begin with a great number of different areas. Start with the basics, and add new areas as you are ready to do so. It is much easier to establish procedures and rules when there are a few important areas well-stocked with exciting activities.

Including too many center areas before you have enough creative jobs to fill them will overwhelm you and invite off-task behavior during center time. Take it slow and plan carefully.

Step Two: Setting Up Your Classroom

Each center should include:

- shelves for holding needed materials and manipulatives
- floor area and table(s) and chairs for workspace
- wall space for displaying charts and student work
- materials to enable completion of the tasks and jobs assigned to the area, such as pencils, crayons, paper, scissors, stapler, tape, date stamp, letter stamps, envelopes, message board, hole punches, etc.

Think through each area you have chosen as a center, and note any materials you think are important to that area. Consider your style of teaching and your students' needs.

For example, in my library or reading center, I like to include a tape recorder with headphones. This is my listening area. However, many teachers highlight this skill, and so they choose to design a center specifically as a listening station. (More specific ideas are included in the chapters on each center area.)

In planning for each center, think first of what you already have in your room. Which centers could use desks pushed together to form a small table as the work space? (Try placing two table legs into a large coffee can when pushing desks or tables together to form a larger surface. This keeps them from constantly sliding apart.)

What centers should include a few isolated desks to form quieter work areas? There are some unique tables designed for special tasks, such as kidney-shaped tables that allow the teacher to sit across from each child.

You will want to utilize any special features your classroom has, and design your centers so that they function well in your particular setting. What shelves already built in to the room must be used to hold certain materials because of the location or size of the shelf? Consider the space you have, and the furniture you need and can obtain, in order to design the classroom that will work for you and your students.

For additional shelf space, check with your principal to see if there are shelves not currently in use either in your building, or in another building in your school district. You might be surprised at what you find. If you can purchase new furniture, shop wisely. Low shelving works well as center dividers, and still allows you to see throughout your classroom. Also, the tops of low-built shelves can be used to display tasks. Double-sided shelving units are perfect to use in centers, and they are less expensive to purchase than two separate shelves.

If you find that you need to provide much of the furniture, don't give up. Check out your basement, garage, or attic. You never know what is tucked away that might be useful if used another way. I have used old coffee tables as work areas for children to use while sitting on the rug.

Visit local thrift shops and garage sales. Check with neighbors and parents of children in your classroom who might be willing to donate old furniture. One year, a student's parent offered to build anything I needed if I would supply the materials. A teacher friend of mine had a parent who had refurnished her child's bedroom, and donated several beautiful bookshelves to her classroom.

Don't feel you have to have a large shelf for every area. Start with whatever you have, and add items gradually as you find a real need. It is probably a bigger mistake to fill your room with too much.

You can always use a bookcase to house a little of everything. Try painting each shelf a different color, and color-coding the items that belong on them to help the children replace materials in the correct spot. Or materials can be placed in different-colored tubs, depending on whether they deal with science, math, or language development. The shelf can have colored stickers to indicate what bins belong where.

This arrangement works well in a very small room. The children can take what they need from the appropriate learning center's shelves and work in a central location, and yet cleanup can be fast, with everyone able to help.

No matter how you set up your classroom, the most important thing is to be well organized. A workable structure within the classroom environment will provide a solid scaffolding to promote learning; and the children will be able to function independently and cooperatively, while learning what they need to know in the way they learn best. They will use the materials to complete your assigned tasks, and then create new learning activities and games for themselves that you never dreamed of! (See Fig. 2-3 for a sample room plan which incorporates learning centers.)

Adjusting Your Room Arrangement

As you proceed with your year, you may encounter difficulties with your center time that can be eliminated with minor changes to the room plan.

• **Too much noise:** Centers that produce much noise, even when children are working on-task, should be placed away from centers that contain quiet work stations. Try moving the quiet center to an out-of-the-way place in the room. Another option is to place a barrier between the noisy area and other centers of the room.

For example, I have my block center in a carpeted corner. It is near the science center, and that works well, for the children in the

(continued on page 32)

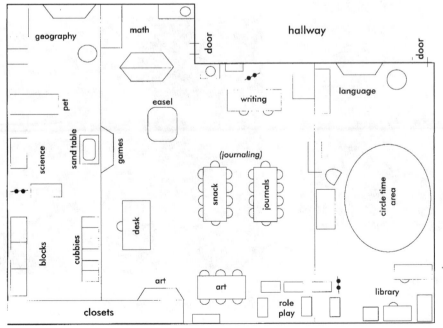

Fig. 2-3 A sample floor plan which incorporates learning centers into the classroom.

Creating Learning Centers

Art Table

The art table is located near shelves that hold art supplies for the children.

Easel

Our classroom has a two-sided easel with room on each side for two children. One side of the easel is devoted to assigned art tasks, while the other side is for art projects of the students' own choice.

Language Center

Lots of activities that allow children to learn about the alphabet and the formation of words and sentences are included in the language center.

Here, a student works with an interactive chart in the language center.

Library Center

The library center is a carpeted, out-of-the-way area with lots of books available for students to read. Here, a student demonstrates a task to Mr. Fox, our principal.

A stand in the library/circle center area can hold Big Books or interactive charts.

This boy is this week's Fabulous Friend; he tells a classmate about photos that he brought from home. The photos will stay in the library center all week.

Role Play Center

The role play center provides play activities related to current thematic units, as well as tasks that allow students to practice writing, math, and social skills in "real-life" settings. Here, the role play center has been turned into a pet store.

Math Center/Geography Center

The math center includes storage areas that contain manipulatives for counting and sorting activities, as well as activities that promote problem-solving and critical-thinking skills.

The geography center, located to the left of the math center, contains lots of mapping activities as well as activities that expose children to literature, music, art, and games from many cultures around the world.

Gross Motor/Block Area

The block area should be out of the way, carpeted, and placed away from walls adjoining other classrooms or centers that require quiet concentration — block areas tend to be very noisy places!

Science Center

The science center has a shelf full of activities, a table with tasks to complete, and a chart stand for poetry or interactive charts. Locating the science center near the windows allows me to use the outside world as a subject for observation.

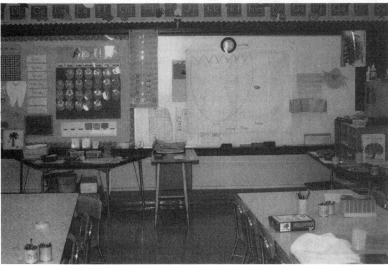

Calendar/Writing Centers

The writing center helps children develop specific writing skills, but also provides them with opportunities for creative expression. Two journal tables are included in the center.

Here, a student completes a calendar math activity in the calendar center (located to the left of the language center in the photo above, left).

These cubbies are made from three nine-compartment shoe organizers, stood on end and lined up. They provide an accessible but out-of-the-way place for children to keep their papers and other belongings.

science center are constantly moving around and discussing their work. Any activity that goes on in the block area can be tolerated by students working in science. I have also placed my cardboard cubbies next to the block center. They cushion the noise, and it provides additional space between the block center and another center that may be next to it.

• **Not enough space to children to work:** Children might need floor or table space, according to the specific tasks they choose in a center. If your room is small, do not fill each center up with furniture. Put a large table near the middle of the room, next to your open

Two children play a memory game in the games center.

floor area. The children can bring work from any center to the table or floor and work alongside children from other areas.

I taught in a modular unit for several years which housed ten small centers. I set the room up in the manner shown in Fig. 2-4. To allow for a quick cleanup, I purchased plastic baskets to hold the activities for each center. The baskets were color-coded to a specific center, so that every child found it easy to help clean up and put things away where they belonged.

• **Constant disruption of children at work by others not in their center:** If children are constantly being disrupted in their work, check how you have positioned your centers. Placing quiet, cognitive centers next to more active social areas might be too much temptation for young children to stay focused on their work.

For example, children working in the art center are often mobile as well as social. Placing the art center in the middle of your room might require children to travel through another center to wash their hands. Their chatter as they create works of art would likely spread to all corners of the room. And carrying dripping glue or paint to a drying area, or to show an adult their work, can create a mess throughout the room. Such an active area should be placed near space needed for drying work, near the sink, and away from any quiet work station.

• **Difficulty with organization of materials within centers:** If your centers are constantly a mess, check to see if you have enough storage space for all materials necessary for the work at that center. Are the materials organized on a shelf, or do they sit out on the work area, so that messes occur and student work gets lost in the materials? Collect old baskets, cardboard shoe cubbies, file holders, and plastic stacking shelves used for mail. Use these to keep work areas neat and materials orderly.

• **Poor traffic patterns:** Do children have to travel through centers to get to their cubbies? Must they move through someone's work area to change centers, wash their hands, get a drink, or use the restroom? No center should be designed around busy traffic routes. Check to see that your shelves and tables are positioned to encourage children to walk around centers, rather than through them.

• **Completed work constantly being misplaced:** Is there a special basket that holds completed work? Is it located near the center of the room with the children's center charts, or where you might be working with children during center time? Placing it in the center of the room allows you as well as other children to note if children put completed work papers away before getting their center chart to change work stations. This also allows you the opportunity to quickly ask if they have remembered to put their name on their papers.

All of these problems can be alleviated by simply redesigning your floor plan. But before you begin to move the furniture around, take a careful look on paper.

Recently, a good friend who teaches a multiage primary class wanted to make some changes before the new school year began. Carla was concerned that the older children returning to her classroom would be bored by the same setup. Carla is an excellent teacher, and knows her students inside and out. However, it always helps to get another point of view.

First, I asked her if the room had worked the year before. Her answer was, mostly yes, but not completely. I suggested that the children would feel comfortable knowing some things had remained constant. Leaving the furniture and center areas in

A view of my classroom. The easel, calendar math, writing, and language centers are on the left; games, art, and role play centers are on the right near the windows.

the same place, but changing several generic jobs, could help them recognize that their work would be expanded this year. I told Carla to think through her floor plan, listing things that worked very well and things that went wrong. If it worked well, she might be inviting trouble changing it just for the sake of change. But if there was a problem, maybe

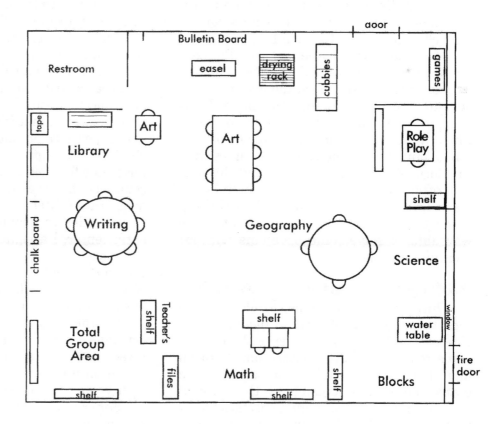

Fig. 2-4 Floor plan for a small, modular classroom.

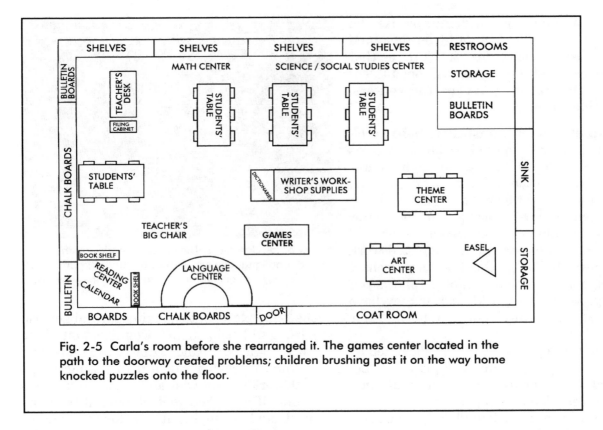

Fig. 2-5 Carla's room before she rearranged it. The games center located in the path to the doorway created problems; children brushing past it on the way home knocked puzzles onto the floor.

she could discover a better arrangement.

The next day, Carla came over set for the year. She had made a few simple changes, and now felt the room was perfect (see Fig. 2-5, 2-6, for Carla's before and after floor plans).

For example, she loved the art area near her sink, so that remained the same. However, she remembered that her daughter Chelsea had spent many an afternoon after school putting away puzzles. The games shelf was located near her doorway, and the puzzles often got knocked off the shelf as the class left in the afternoon. By thinking through what worked and what didn't, Carla was able to solve some problems without creating new ones.

Adding New Centers to Your Plan

Once you feel you're ready to add new centers, there are lots of ways to include them. The easiest is simply to observe the centers you already have in your classroom. Notice if any of them always takes your students an entire center time to complete the work. If so, you may have too many expectations for that one area. Think of ways you can break

that center into two different stations. What tasks would work well together, and be challenging and interesting enough to maintain the children's enthusiasm for that area?

I went through this several years ago. My art area consisted of a large table for specific art projects, a smaller table for "free" art experiences with materials such as play dough and paper scraps, and the easel. Too often, children would go to the art center and not have time for each task. So, my two art tables remained the art center, and the easel became a separate center.

In order to provide some choice in the easel center, I assigned one side of the easel to a specific task, while the other side contained different materials and could be used as the child wished. I later got a larger easel, with two places for painting on each side.

Another way to try out a new center is by setting up a temporary center based on the interests of your students. If it sustains their attention and can be easily assimilated into your room, it can become permanent.

For example, you could open an inventions center during a unit on simple machines or

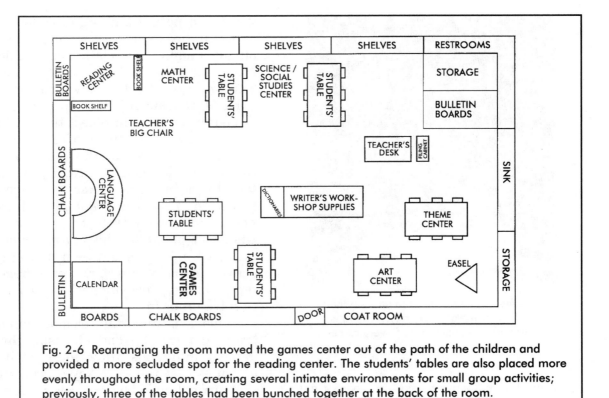

Fig. 2-6 Rearranging the room moved the games center out of the path of the children and provided a more secluded spot for the reading center. The students' tables are also placed more evenly throughout the room, creating several intimate environments for small group activities; previously, three of the tables had been bunched together at the back of the room.

transportation. The students could design and build simple inventions, constructing them with recycled materials, wood scraps, Legos™, or some other materials donated by students and local hardware stores. They could then write about their inventions' value, send away for a patent, and present their inventions to the class in order to promote their use.

If this area becomes popular, the class might ask to keep it going throughout the year. They could continue to invent products useful in other thematic units, such as weather gauges, solar vehicles, water-powered engines, or new uses of compost. The enthusiasm of the students determines whether or not the center becomes a permanent part of the classroom.

Another method for introducing a new center is to test it within an already existing center. My geography center is an example. It began as a portion of our science center. Each month, I created manipulative experiences to teach the children about people and places around the world. I started with only a few materials and books, and spent a year creating and locating enough activities to open a geography center the following year.

I was relieved to take this project slowly. It made it fun, rather than an overwhelming responsibility. Seven years later, my geography center continues to evolve as I change my focus from one particular country within a continent to another. But my young students still love to make maps and flags and study the habitats of their favorite animals. They love to play with the toys of children from other parts of the world. And together, we love the excellent books that teach us the folk tales and legends of other cultures.

Specific Activities in Centers

The activities in each area change throughout the year. It is most important to remember that each center should include numerous activities at a variety of developmental levels, in order to provide a developmentally appropriate environment for each student.

Books should be included in every center to demonstrate how they relate to our everyday lives. Joke books can be placed in the games center; number and shape books can be in the

I have the children stamp the date on their journals after making an entry. Writing is a very important component of every center.

math center; coloring books and books with interesting illustrations can go in the art center; fiction and nonfiction books can be housed in science, geography, and language centers.

Writing should also be included in every center, for the experience of writing individualizes the instruction for each child. As children write, they reflect upon their own prior knowledge in order to assimilate or accommodate new information they have investigated. This reflective writing allows them to understand what they know, building the metacognitive skills they need in order to utilize their new knowledge.

I strongly believe that young children should have consistent opportunities to reread their own writing. Every time a young child writes, ensure that he can share his work with another person. In this way, he learns the power of literacy, and practices such skills as editing his own work and reading text with his own vocabulary, repeating activities specific to his stage of development.

Types of Activities

I have two main types of activities to complete in each center: specific tasks, which are jobs the children must do when working at the center; and work jobs, which are more generic in nature and are designed to offer opportunities to practice specific skills I have already taught to the class. The specific tasks come and go as students complete the work. The work jobs tend to stay for much longer periods of time in order to give children numerous chances to repeat the activities.

More specific examples of center tasks and jobs for each area of the room are given throughout the book, particularly in the chapters discussing each center area. Again, the "must do" tasks come and go, and are connected in some way to the thematic unit whenever possible. This allows students to make connections between concepts and across curricular areas, and encourages better use of the information when it comes time to solve problems.

This is an important element in an integrated curriculum. The jobs using the more generic materials allow for repetition of activities that reinforce key concepts within the curriculum. They are never designed to introduce a specific skill, but to reinforce a curricular objective that has already been taught. They should begin with the use of manipulatives, but opportunities to transfer the concept to abstract form should be available when students are ready.

For example, addition problems would be introduced by having the children count beads, then having them color those beads on paper, and finally by having them write the problems in number form.

Children sort and count their m&m's for their graph. Each uses a different technique, one counting and marking the chart, the other placing candies on the graph.

Math Center Activity

This week, each child must complete one specific task: a bracelet made from a pipe cleaner and beads. The activity provides an opportunity to assess the children's patterning and counting skills. In a primary classroom, you might ask that they design their bracelet in an ABCD pattern, using a total of 20 beads. When they finish, they must write how many times they had to repeat their pattern in order to have the 20 beads.

For a more challenging task, design a more difficult problem. The children must use only 20 beads, but can choose from only three colors. What patterns can they create? Place a graph in the learning center showing the patterns the children created.

As a follow-up activity, divide the class into cooperative groups to discover how many different patterns it's possible to create with 20 beads and three colors. Many activities like this are open-ended, leaving the choice of pattern to the individual child.

Along with this pattern task are numerous other materials that each child can work with. He can:

- sort and classify postage stamps from a small plastic container
- make additional patterns with Unifix ™ cubes, beads, and tiles

- investigate sets of numerals using beads and cups (found in *Math Their Way*)
- seriate bottles of seeds from the least full to the most
- seriate mittens, shells, insects, or trucks (depending on the thematic unit) from the smallest to the largest
- count change according to the number of days the child has been in school (Example: on the 25th day of school, the child can use coins to count to 25 — one quarter, or two dimes and a nickel, or five nickels, etc.)

I assign the number of jobs that the children must complete. It is each child's responsibility to choose jobs which encourage her math development. I monitor her progress, assessing her completed work, reteaching when necessary, and directing her to try a specific job when she hasn't tackled a job she should have attempted.

Many of the materials stay in the center for the entire year (Unifix™ cubes, money, beads, junk boxes, tiles . . .), but the tasks the children complete with them increase in difficulty.

Chapter 3

Managing Center-Oriented Classrooms

When you delegate responsibility to children you share your power. You do this because you are confident in your own ability to learn and you know that children need to practice taking responsibility in order to become more proficient and powerful learners themselves. When you delegate responsibility you take the most fundamental step in establishing the structured classroom.

— Donald H. Graves,
Build a Literate Classroom

hen I first began using centers, I found everything overwhelming. My problem was typical: I was trying to create a new environment without letting go of some old habits. My classroom structure remained on the exterior, like that crustacean, while I allowed the children to wiggle about within the confined space of old guidelines. This allowed for little experimentation in learning and little risk-taking in responsibility and decision-making.

To encourage students to take more responsibility for the classroom and their learning, you must give up some control. You must share the authority with your students. If you want them to make decisions on their own, you must allow them to have freedom of choice and the freedom to make mistakes. This does not mean giving up your authority in the classroom or letting the children do whatever they choose, whenever they choose. Allow students the freedom to make choices in their learning, but hold them accountable for their work. Your internal structure provides the security and confidence children need in order to take risks in their learning.

The most common remark made by visitors in my classroom is how self-directed and self-sufficient my students are. This is no accident. I take a great deal of time at the beginning of the year teaching my students how to take responsibility for their own learning. We form the habits necessary for learning to take place. When the children discover that they can be successful learning on their own, the intrinsic motivation and personal responsibility occur naturally.

I can then trust each child to work to develop inner controls and incentives for achieving at his own maximum potential. How much I can trust each child and how often I need to step in is very individualized. These decisions are made continuously throughout the year as I monitor the work and work habits of my students.

For example, when Christa spends most of her time in the language center talking, playing teacher and imitating my group lessons, I allow her to do so. She is reinforcing her knowledge of letter recognition and sounds. But when it's time to warn the class that center time will end in ten minutes, I also whisper to Christa that she now needs to sit down with the letter task and complete her work.

As Demiko chooses to go to the block center because his best friend is there, I remind him that he has a job to complete in the science center. I might ask him if he would like to go to science first, then choose blocks. Or I might simply remind him that his science task must be completed by a certain day. But if that completion date is very close and Demiko has been putting off the task for some time, I will most likely insist that he go first to the science center, assuring him that he will be allowed to go to blocks when he has completed his obligations in science. And then I make certain that there is room for him at the block center when he is ready to work there. These are subtle lessons I give throughout the year, instructing my young students in how to make wise decisions about their learning.

Once you decide to relinquish your teacher-centered classroom to create a child-centered environment, you begin to make decisions about what you can give up and teach the children to control. You rethink your day and find ways to give authority to your students. You put materials such as staplers, date stamps, and tape out around the room, so that the children can solve their own problems with torn papers or book pages that need assembling. You learn to count to five or ten or fifteen, watching rather than jumping in, as Michael negotiates a problem with Adam. You begin to teach children how to learn, rather than what to learn.

I model the process of learning, and help the children discover how to find answers to their questions without coming to me. I provide the scaffolding when children are ready to move forward, either by working with them myself, or providing an opportunity for a cooperative learning activity between two or more children who work well together and support each other's learning. I create the environment, lay the foundation so that the children know how to function in that environment, create meaningful experiences to support the lessons I teach them, then allow them to go about their work practicing these skills. I monitor their process and progress, encouraging them to take risks with new work and redirecting their efforts when all does not go well. I introduce new materials and new concepts as the children show a readiness to progress in their skills, modeling carefully how to use new equipment and complete new tasks.

Laying the Foundation

Children cannot be expected to take the responsibility for their own learning overnight. The teacher must take them into this process gradually, first teaching them how to take responsibility for little tasks, like putting work where it belongs when it is finished. Every task that your children are able to accomplish on their own should become their responsibility. This is a key point in making your centers run smoothly. It is important for three reasons:

1. The children will gain a tremendous amount of self-respect as they realize that their teacher trusts them to be responsible for these tasks, and that they are successful at accomplishing them.

2. As the children take on these responsibilities, they begin to take more ownership in the materials in their classroom. Fewer items are lost or broken, and the children even begin to help each other take care of the classroom. The process of taking ownership in their classroom brings the group closer together, fostering a community of learners.

3. Any job that they do for themselves is one less job that you will need to do. That allows the teacher more class time to teach and more time, when the students are not there, for planning new activities.

You need to take some time to consider what responsibilities you will be comfortable giving away to your students. For example, some teachers allow their students to correct their own or others' work. That is not something I'm comfortable giving up to my young students. I like to see firsthand how each child has accomplished her work, and I like to ask her questions as she shows me her completed assignments.

I have my students read their writing to me, for it is through rereading their own writing that children often learn to read. Ongoing, individual assessments allow me opportunities to take anecdotal records and reteach any misinformation immediately.

I *am* comfortable with allowing each child to choose his work station. I like him to take the responsibility for determining what he is able to accomplish well in a day, budgeting

After these kindergartners write in their journals, they will read what they have written to me.

his time, and accomplishing work that I've assigned. Each teacher must make his own decisions on what he can allow his students to control, and what he feels he must continue to govern.

As you begin your year, take the time to teach cooperative learning strategies and individual responsibility. It is vital in order to build trust in your classroom and create a community of learners. You must help the children develop habits of learning: staying at one task until it is completed; choosing new work when a job is finished; talking through a problem when difficulties arise; and repeating activities to ensure mastery of concepts. When this is done carefully, teachers discover they gain more by giving up the control. When students have been given instruction in how to learn and allowed lots of time to form good learning habits, center time runs smoothly, freeing the teacher for conferencing, working with small groups, assessing skills in an authentic and ongoing context, reteaching, and encouraging skill development.

The First Weeks

Let me walk you through my first few weeks of school, as I show how I go about creating my child-centered environment without totally losing control.

I begin my year with just a few centers open. Only those centers in which the children can manage their activity with little direction are available to them the first week. Furthermore, these centers are not filled completely with activities. I place only those tasks that all children will recognize and accomplish on their own, with little explanation and interference from me:

- The role play center is a housekeeping area, with baby dolls, dishes, play food, and a telephone.
- The library is filled with alphabet and wordless picture books.
- The math center is filled with tubs of manipulatives for free exploration.
- The art area has paper for children to produce their first self-portrait, and playdough for creative art experiences.

Week One

Before center time begins each day, I introduce one or two new centers. In this way, the children are gradually introduced to each work station in our classroom. For example, the following are introductory lessons that might occur during the first week of center time:

MONDAY: Read the book *Block City*, by Robert Louis Stevenson. Discuss rules that are needed for the block center.

Example: "Put blocks away on the shelf in the appropriate place so that each shape may be found as you build."

Example: "Plan a building by looking at books in the center, build the building, then draw a picture of your completed work."

TUESDAY: Give instructions for tasks at the writing center. These might include: how to practice handwriting by writing your name on folded paper; writing letters or words on the dry wipe or chalkboard; creating words with magnetic letters and copying them onto the board or paper; completing the papers marked, "I like Kindergarten!"

WEDNESDAY: Read a book, such as *Mr. Gumpy's Outing*, by John Burningham, and give instructions for completing the transportation tasks and activities at the science center.

THURSDAY: Read the book *School Bus*, by Donald Crews, and model the steps that should be taken when painting at the easel. Demonstrate how to paint a bus using geometric shapes such as rectangles, circles, and squares.

FRIDAY: Lead a discussion about how people use reading and writing every day at home. Elicit such ideas as:

• reading cookbooks
• writing invitations to a birthday party
• reading the newspaper or magazines
• writing phone messages

Filling a math center with manipulatives for counting activities is a good addition for the first weeks.

Have a variety of literacy materials on hand to place in the center as the children make their suggestions. Examples might include telephone books, message pads and pencils, a calendar, newspapers and magazines, cookbooks for kids, party invitations, and stationery and envelopes. Use the children's ideas when placing literacy materials in the role play center. Tell the children they should use reading and writing each time they work in this center.

After each lesson, center time begins. I quickly assign groups of children to a center, and they remain there for approximately ten minutes. The point of this short center time is to teach the children to stay in the center they are in, putting materials away as tasks are completed and trying a variety of jobs without changing to a different area. I am not yet keeping track of where each child works.

The number of children in each center will depend on how many centers you have open and how many children are in your class. Specific limitations on how many children will be allowed to work in each center will be determined later, when all center areas have been introduced. For now, center time must be short, for the children's attention span is not long, and the centers do not have an abundance of activities to choose from.

It is important not to overdo center time, for you want to avoid getting into bad habits.

Go to a center, try some jobs, clean up, and center time is over. At this point, you are simply introducing the children to the concept of working independently in a designated center.

Each day, new centers are introduced. As the children begin to accept the idea of staying at their center to try new tasks, center time can be lengthened gradually. When all centers are opened, the cycle begins again, introducing new activities into each existing center. At this time of year, the materials introduced are less thematic in nature, and tend to be more generic, such as Unifix™ cubes, scales, the stapler, and hole punches. Soon there are more activities for the children to choose from when they go to each center. It becomes necessary to lengthen center time, for you will be encouraging the children to stay in the center and try each job, some that are new and some that have been there and they have tried before. As the children repeat the activity, they will get better and better at accomplishing it.

For example, alphabet puzzles and Unifix™ cubes should be used again and again throughout the year. You are teaching the children to try new tasks and repeat old tasks. They are forming good habits for learning, repeating activities in order to master specific skills, taking risks with new tasks, making predictions about their work and confirming or denying those predictions, and discussing their work with their peers. They are practicing their ability to stay on-task and communicate with others as they learn. Monitoring their work in the centers will allow you to recognize how and when to lengthen the time spent in centers and which centers should have more tasks introduced.

This process is considerably easier if your children have worked in an environment such as this in the past, or if you have a portion of your students for more than one year, as in a multiage classroom. When half to two-thirds of your students are returning to the same environment, they become good role models for the new students. Utilize their experience, for children often learn better from their peers than from an adult.

It is important to review the stages I am defining *every year*. Multiage teachers have often agreed with me during inservices that they must go over the procedures each year, so that all children in the class hear the rules together. Having the children take responsibility for the implementation of your classroom procedures enhances the caring community you need to establish with each new group of students.

To help young children recall where each center is located in the room, include a picture with the name of the center in each location. These pictures can correspond to a picture on your center chart. With a group that has a great deal of difficulty staying on-task at centers, you might even take photos of children in the classroom at work in each center. Hang them near the materials; for instance, you could hang a photograph of a child completing a journal entry near the journals, so that each child can visualize just what his responsibility is for this task.

Keeping Track of Center Activity

After approximately two to three weeks, the children should be working well in centers for approximately fifteen to twenty minutes. You can now introduce tasks in your first curriculum-based thematic unit. This is a good time to introduce some type of chart or contract that will help the children make wise choices about which center to choose to complete work in each day, as well as helping you to keep track of who has accomplished each task.

Center charts or contracts can be designed to meet your needs. (Charts simply document the child's work choices, while contracts involve the child in promising to complete specific tasks. The latter become more individualized.)

The center chart in Fig. 3-1 simply tells you and the student what center he or she has been to. It is easily used with young children, as they learn to match the center names to the printed word on the chart and as posted within the center.

The contract in Fig. 3-2 can be used with any age, and is more flexible. Before photocopying the contracts for each week, write the tasks to be accomplished on the chart, so they will appear on each child's contract. Once the child's name has been written on the contract, jobs specific to each child can be added individually by the teacher or the student. This is particularly nice in multiage and/or inclusion classrooms, where tasks will likely vary for each child. As the child works in each center, the day can be documented.

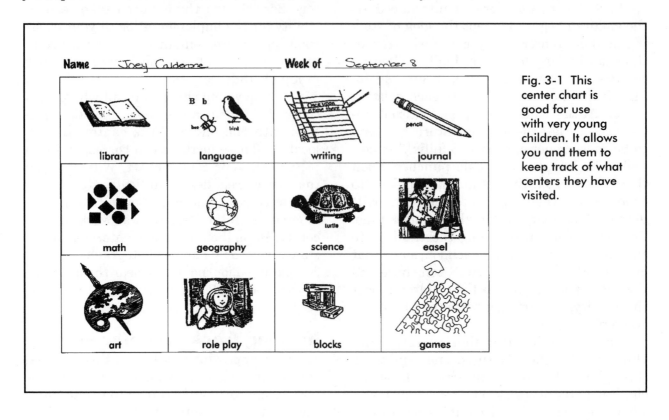

Fig. 3-1 This center chart is good for use with very young children. It allows you and them to keep track of what centers they have visited.

Fig. 3-2 This is a very flexible contract which can be used with children of any age. It provides a lot of specific information on each child's work in every center.

Notations can be made on a child's chart before he visits the center by writing what he should accomplish, or as the child asks to change centers. On the chart in Fig. 3-3 the child reported what work she had completed. This technique helps children stay on-task and allows them opportunities to reflect upon their work.

Charts can also be designed to show each child's work over an entire month. Carla Amburgey finds many advantages to this approach (see her chart in Fig. 3-4). Reproducible copies of charts 3-1 through 3-4 are on pages 165-168.

Teaching the children to use these charts, as they become aware of accomplishing specific tasks in each center, has worked well for me. It is not difficult, for the children are usually ready to have some sort of written documentation that they can refer to in order to recall what they have accomplished and what still needs to be done. You may want to mark the charts for your students; or you may feel your students are capable of marking their own. That is a decision best made by each teacher.

Charts are also helpful to use with parents. As fewer paper-pencil tasks come home, these charts show anxious parents what work is going on in their child's classroom. They are assured that you are monitoring the activity time. During conferences, they are useful in showing what centers are chosen first each week by their child — and which are put off until the last moment. The charts document the process and its importance in your classroom.

Progressing in Center Time

When the children are working well in one center for a period of twenty minutes or more, and they are accustomed to utilizing the charts that keep track of their work, they are ready for additional center time. This usually occurs soon after you introduce your chart system. The idea is to stretch

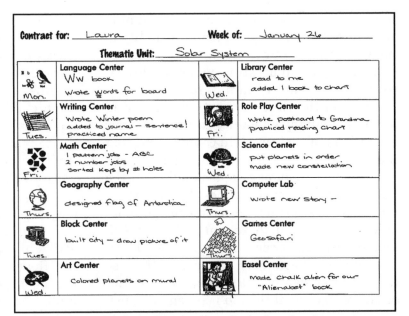

Fig. 3-3 Students use this chart to report what they have accomplished in each center.

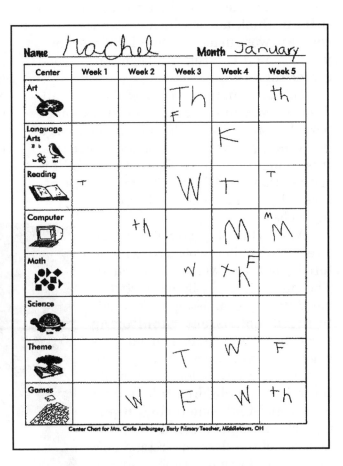

Fig. 3-4 This center chart created by Carla Amburgey, an early primary teacher in Middletown, Ohio, allows her to track each child's work over an entire month's time.

your independent work time to a minimum of 50 minutes. This allows more flexibility in time-on-task as your center activities become more complex and the number of choices within each center continues to grow.

Around the third or fourth week of center time, I simply announce to the class how proud I am of their work in centers, and that they will now work in two centers each day. For the next week or two, depending on the class, I have two center times. I assign them into their first center, to make this go more quickly. We work in these centers for approximately fifteen to twenty minutes, then I give five minutes warning before cleanup time, so that children can plan to complete activities or clean up early if the job is extensive, such as in the block area. I then turn out the lights to announce it is time for them to clean up, come to the rug, and choose their next center. As they clean up their work, I remind them to think about which center they will choose to work in next. When all children have joined me on our rug, we begin our second center time.

This stage of the process teaches the children to work in one center for an extended period of time, but to clean up and choose a new center when they have accomplished this. It is an important part of the process, for it is critical that the children learn to work extensively at one center before making a change.

When this step is well emphasized, fewer children need to be monitored about their work in each center. The child who is easily distracted or has difficulty completing tasks tends to need consistent monitoring throughout the year. It is not an overwhelming task when you only have to monitor a few children. After all, these are the children who would need consistent monitoring in any type of environment. And when the majority of the class understand how to function in center time, they are quick to encourage others to complete several tasks before moving on to another work station.

The importance of developing the habit of staying in each center and trying a variety of tasks cannot be overstated. It makes the difference between well-run center activity and confusion. Center time must be productive for each child. In order for this to take place on an individual basis for each child, she must be taught to try new tasks, repeat "old" activities for reinforcement, and communicate with her peers in group collaborative learning experiences. The repetition of generic activities, completed in the context of different thematic units, serves to reinforce specific skills in a playful environment.

Repeating tasks that promote the acquisition of specific skills in a variety of thematic units also allows the child to make important connections between the skill and how it is used in everyday life. This encourages her to utilize these skills in her daily work, and promotes meaningful, purposeful work, rather than meaningless, mindless skill and drill.

Connecting specific ideas to a variety of general topics also allows the brain to make the connections the child needs in order to apply the knowledge. When a child brings meaning to a task and understands a purpose for the work she involves herself in, real learning occurs.

Activities involving children in self-discovery, the responsibility to choose the

Changing centers. One child discusses the choice of his next center with me, while another child waits her turn to talk to me, and a third child looks for his center chart.

work they will complete in a day, and the expectation that they will take the responsibility for their learning and for their classroom, are what allows the center approach to empower children to be in charge of their own learning. Each element makes a subtle but critical difference. When your students feel they control their learning and experience success with that role, they will be intrinsically motivated to do their best and to take risks in their learning.

Individual Choice in Making Center Changes

It will become obvious to you when the children are ready to move on to the final element of this individualized learning time. This important aspect involves deciding for themselves when they are ready to change centers. As the children move into completing tasks designed around your curriculum, some centers will demand more time than others. Soon you will see that children in some centers need to change earlier than children in other areas. Some tasks will require children to become more involved in the work and take additional time to complete an assignment well. Some centers, such as science and math, soon consist of a multitude of jobs to choose, besides the specific, regularly assigned theme-based task.

Typically, one to two weeks after you've doubled your center time, the children will notice that the assigned amount of time is either too long or too short. They are working well, but the time element is not working for them. Begin center time with a class meeting to discuss this problem. Help the children discover for themselves how to solve this problem. When someone suggests, as he always does, that he would like to decide when he should change, ask the children how to make this work. Let them solve the problem and develop a plan that allows them to take the responsibility of completing tasks within a center, cleaning up their materials, and making the decision to change to another area.

At this time, I usually set limits on how many children will be allowed to work in each

Here, four children work cooperatively in the block area to build a zoo.

area at a time. We discuss this as a class, but I initiate the responses I need by noting such specifics as how much room will be needed in blocks to build, and how many chairs are in art, etc., so no center will hold too many children at one time. I also suggest that we set a specific number of generic jobs that must be completed before making any center change. Usually, it begins with the assigned task and three activities. Then the children may choose to get their charts, bring them to you (or an aide or volunteer), and choose their next center. This is an exciting time, for the children realize how much responsibility they have been given.

As you can imagine, some take the responsibility with more care than others. It is somewhat like allowing children to wander through a candy store with an open bag. Expect the children to take a few steps backward for a week or so. You will have to be available to monitor their work, taking on the role of the "mean teacher" in some instances as you demand that they go back to where they were and complete the task with more care, or try additional jobs. The strict adherence to this policy is crucial at this time, for their independent decision-making habits are being formed. It will not take a long time, if you are consistent and demanding, to reinforce the idea that the rules will be enforced. If the centers are filled with appropriate materials, tasks that engage them in real learning, and activities that promote the understanding that they have control of their learning, the children will do better than you expect. My kindergartners always amaze me at how well they accept this responsibility. Lay the foundation carefully, plan the environment around their needs, and trust that they will rise to the occasion!

I have had groups of children who move into this format well, but the process deteriorated along the way for some reason. They might be too competitive, trying to complete tasks before other children. They might be emotionally tied to working with a friend and want to hurry through work in order to move to a center with that person. There are a variety of reasons that the system breaks down. This doesn't happen often, but I have experienced it. In this instance, I simply moved backward to the stage where we completed one center, cleaned up together, and then came to the rug to choose the second center. This was not fun for them, and they received the message that they have to be able to handle the responsibility in order to keep the privilege of self-determination.

I was astonished at how quickly the class responded to this setback. I chose to continue in this manner for two solid weeks. One week was necessary to reaffirm the habit of trying a variety of tasks and completing them with care; one was added to make the point that if they do not accept the responsibility, I will step in and take it for them. When this occurred, the problem completely disappeared. The lesson was a difficult one for my children and they were determined that they would not have to learn it again.

This entire process, learning how to work in centers and making individual choices independently, takes approximately four to five weeks. By the end of the first month of school, my kindergartners are working through an hour of center time, completing tasks, and choosing new work. Some days they may work in three centers, some days they may stay in one center for the entire hour.

I have worked with many teachers as they move into this type of center time. Most are concerned that their students will want to change centers constantly. They envision their days will be spent forcing children to stay in an area to complete work. However, they normally find just the opposite is true. When children feel comfortable about the rules and procedures in which they work, and centers are stocked with work the children find important and challenging, they will work independently within this structure for long periods of time.

Completing the Charts or Contracts

Completing charts or contracts is helpful for determining what needs to be accomplished and what work should be completed. When a center or task is completed, it is marked on the chart. It is our class's goal for every child to visit every center each week. Teachers often ask me if I allow a child to visit a center twice in one week, even when he has not yet worked in all the centers. This is an excellent question. My answer is, "Yes — occasionally." There are several reasons that it can be important for a child to repeat a center in one week.

When a child has not completed work in a center, but center time is over, he simply

When a center or task is completed, it is marked on the chart. It is our class's goal for every child to visit every center each week.

brings me his work. I clip it to the charts so that we will remember it the next day. He is allowed to go back to that center first thing the next day to complete the task. This will not happen often if you allow enough time in your day for center time, and if you are careful to give enough warning before beginning to clean up. Children hear that warning and know it is time to focus their attention on completing their work.

There are also instances of children wanting to return to a center for additional practice or an opportunity to repeat a task. For example, a child might wish to make a second version of a book in the writing center, or repeat a patterning activity in math. Do I allow her to skimp on one area in order to practice another more extensively? Again, the answer is specific to the child and the situation. When a child's request is legitimate and her interest is focused on that skill, I usually honor her need to repeat that activity. I always explain my decision to her, so that she understands that I have bent the rules because of her desire to learn. This helps build a sense of respect and trust that I value the children's individual needs.

What about the centers they miss? I don't believe their education will suffer greatly by skipping one center for one week. Actually, I doubt that the work they would accomplish there would be so beneficial if it were forced upon them at a time when some other skill was on their mind.

I can think of numerous examples of this occurring, particularly in our journal and writing centers. By mid-year, many children have discovered their ability to communicate in writing. I recall Joseph working for three straight days in the writing center as he completed his version of *It Didn't Frighten Me!* Another year, Jeff fell in love with the journaling process, completing page after page of intricate drawings with detailed text using inventive spelling strategies, beginning grammatical marks, and even trying some dialogue as his self-confidence in his literacy skills grew. And one group of children were so intrigued with the Unifix™ cubes, they worked in self-organized cooperative learning groups

creating activities to challenge the class in number skills, patterning, and sets.

Creating this environment allows you to make professional judgments specific to each child. It allows flexibility and adjustments as needed for a wide variety of situations. I have found that when I honor a child's real need to deviate from the normal rule of operation, she respects that privilege and uses it wisely. I seldom have problems with children choosing to repeat centers too often, for they enjoy the variety of work set out for them, and they learn to make wise choices.

Activities and Tasks in Centers

In my classroom, I have a variety of activities that support the learning of every child. These are the generic work jobs they can choose, and can be repeated whenever the child visits that center. Examples include:

- picture story cards for children to sequence and use to retell favorite stories
- junk boxes for sorting and classifying, counting, and patterning
- magnetic letters for building letter recognition skills and inventive spelling strategies

The child does not complete all of these activities each time he visits the center, however. These tasks are there for long periods of time, in order to allow for repetition and practice. As some children become proficient with these materials, they will scaffold the learning for others who are working at the activity with them.

Another way to emphasize the need to accomplish several tasks within one center before moving on is to adapt your center chart. I have found that this works well when the problem is a lack of role models for the appropriate behaviors. For example, if you have a situation where the role models are those children who tend to get off-task or do not complete work with care or self-initiative, you might need to force the process on paper. The center chart in Fig. 3-5 (reproducible on page 169) is one I adapted from my picture chart to use with a group that was consistently having difficulty completing work in centers.

Some children wanted to rush through the tasks while others simply wanted to avoid the work altogether. I found myself spending too much time policing the process rather than having opportunities to work with small groups and individuals. On this chart, the children had to mark what jobs they had chosen to complete before they could change centers. The " * jobs" are those assigned tasks that each child had to do, while the others (2 job, 3 job, 4 job) are choice jobs from the shelf. I was also able to indicate when I expected certain choices to be made, such as: reading content area books while working in science and geography; working with a mapping activity, such as a puzzle or matching game, in geography; writing in their journals at the writing center; and including writing in the work at the art, block, and easel centers.

Using this chart was quite interesting for me. I expected the transition to be difficult and unappreciated, but the children surprised me. Those who needed more direction relaxed and got more accomplished independently, while those children who had been quietly self-directed appreciated the fact that I had more time for them and fewer distractions from their nonfocused peers.

Observing this reinforced my belief in how much children *want* adults to set limits for them. My "wild ones" obviously felt comforted and protected when I gave them less room to roam. The tighter boundary allowed them to feel safe enough to trust themselves to work independently and make choices in their work.

I also have specific tasks that come and go with more frequency in each center. These are the tasks that each child *must* do when working in the center. Once the year is underway and center time is running well, every center contains a task that each child must do. The type of job varies and the time element will change, but every center has tasks specific to that area that must be accomplished by each child. It is up to the child whether he completes the assigned task first and then chooses to try two or three activities, or accomplishes the "practice" activities first, building up to completing the assigned task.

The specific tasks do not have to be the same for each child, although they can be. Particularly in multiage and inclusive classrooms, the tasks might be child-specific, or they might be the same task, but structured differently, so that each child can complete the activity at her own level of development.

For example, a book project might be

Fig. 3-5 Use this chart to help children keep on track if they have trouble staying on task or finishing their work.

given on blank paper for more advanced children to complete independently, but pages with some of the text printed on them could be included in some of the books for children who need their literacy development scaffolded, or who may be having difficulty with fine motor development.

Difficult tasks can be placed in centers as options for all children to attempt. Books of varying ability levels are placed on the shelves for children to read, so that some children will be completing "easy readers," while others are retelling wordless picture book stories, and still others completing chapter books. The teacher helps each child choose the appropriate level in which to complete the activity.

Keeping track of task completion is an important aspect of this arrangement, just as it is in a traditional setting. I assess the children's work in several ways:

1. I have the children show me their completed work immediately. This is particularly true at the beginning of the year, as we form habits of learning and working. I have already stated that I have each child read aloud any writing he does. This happens as I monitor center activities, hold small-group and individual conferences, assess skill development and reteach skills, and change centers.

    Classroom assistants and adult volunteers can be invaluable during this portion of the day. I have had the advantage of working with wonderful classroom aides. They enhanced the program more than I could ever explain. I have also run centers alone; it is possible. But it's obviously much easier to operate a program with a consistent, child-centered adult to help listen to children read, change centers, and help solve problems.

2. My classroom contains a large basket in which the children place their completed work. It holds everything except paintings and gluey artwork which has to dry. At the end of the day, I go through the basket, recheck each task, and write whatever notes I need in my assessment notebook. I

consider the process as well as the product: Did the child follow directions, need additional help, or complete the activity in ways I need to recall, such as repeatedly using vowel sounds in inventive spellings? I then either put the work in the child's cubby to take home, or place it in her portfolio for future use.

Whatever your methods of assessment, you simply accommodate how the children give the work to you (in spurts rather than as a whole group). Set a time limit, in terms of days or weeks, for the task to be completed, give the children notice before the time is up, and then assign the child who has not yet completed the task to that center as the final day arrives.

In other words, I give the child every opportunity to complete the tasks in her own time. When that time is up, I step in, and her right to choose a center is lost until the task is completed.

3. I place certain jobs in the centers in order to teach the children responsibility. In this case, I give the children ample opportunities to complete the task, warn them that the job will disappear from the center in two days, then one day, and then . . . it disappears. Any child who has not chosen to complete it does not get to complete it. As my goal here is to teach responsibility, this should be a task that is difficult but

Completed work goes into a special basket.

enjoyable. The completed project should be one the child would want to take home to Mom.

When I have warned that the job will disappear and it does, the children who have not completed the task are astounded. They learn the hard way that when I give a warning, I will follow through. This lesson is a great one to give at the beginning of the year. It is usually effective, and I seldom have difficulties encouraging children to complete tasks. Again, when I do have difficulties with a child, I simply assign the child to the appropriate center, and see that he completes the assigned task first.

4. I also have tasks in some centers that the children must do each week. These tasks do not always have to be formally assessed, but are simply monitored from time to time to gauge progress. For example, at my writing center, all children must practice handwriting once they complete the creative writing task. At the beginning of the year, they accomplish this by practicing to write their own first name.

Toward the middle of the year, the children begin to write their own first and last names. By spring, they choose three friends' names and practice those (Fig 3-6). This allows the children to read and write other names and letters, and breaks up the monot-

ony of writing their own name several times. This task may be accomplished on folded blank paper or lined, according to the need and level of the child. It is wise to offer a variety of materials for the task.

As each person completes the task and shows her paper to me, I take a moment to work on any letters formed incorrectly. Once that is done, the child can put the paper in her cubby and take it home. Papers such as this, done regularly, are not saved each time. I simply document the progress made as the year goes by. What each teacher chooses to keep or send home after a quick check is an individual decision, no different than if the classroom were run traditionally.

Teacher Resources

Brainard, Audrey, and Wrubel, Denise H. *Literature-Based Science Activities: An Integrated Approach.* New York: Scholastic, 1993.

Eisele, Beverly. *Managing the Whole Language Classroom.* Cypress: CA, 1991.

Graves, Donald H. *Build a Literate Classroom.* Portsmouth, NH: Heinemann, 1991.

Kentucky Department of Education. *Primary Thoughts: Implementing Kentucky's Primary Program.* Frankfort, KY: Kentucky Department of Education, 1993.

Politano, Colleen, and Davies, Anne. *Multi-Age and More.* Winnipeg: Peguis Publishers, 1994.

Children's Trade Books

Burningham, John. *Mr. Gumpy's Outing.* New York: Henry Holt and Company, 1970.

Cole, Joanna. *The Magic School Bus: Lost Inside the Solar System.* New York: Scholastic, 1990.

Crews, Donald. *School Bus.* New York: Puffin Books, 1984.

Goss, Janet L., and Harste, Jerome C. *It Didn't Frighten Me!* Worthington, OH: Willowisp Press, 1985.

Hines, Anna Grossnickle. *Sky All Around.* New York: Clarion, 1989.

Stevenson, Robert Louis. *Block City* (illustrated by Ashley Wolff). New York: Puffin Books, 1988.

Winter, Jeanette. *Follow the Drinking Gourd.* New York: The Trumpet Club, 1988.

Fig. 3-6 Having children learn to write their friends' names is a fun way for them to practice their spelling and lettering skills.

CD-ROM

The Magic School Bus Explores the Solar System. Microsoft Corp., 1994.

Chapter 4

Thematic Planning

The brain is designed to perceive and generate patterns, and it resists having meaningless patterns imposed upon it. "Meaningless" patterns are isolated pieces of information unrelated to what makes sense to a student. When the brain's natural capacity to integrate information is acknowledged and invoked in teaching, then vast amounts of initially unrelated or seemingly random information and activities can be presented and assimilated.

— Renate Nummela Caine and Geoffrey Caine, *Teaching and the Human Brain*

he first thing I like to do in June, when my classroom is cleaned up and all the activities are put away, is plan my thematic units for the coming year. I come home from my classroom vowing to keep thoughts of school and teaching out of my head for two solid weeks, but it never happens. I sit down, put my feet up, and my brain starts to review the year, immediately jumping into revising the program. I know this sounds like I have no life — I do. Really. But I find that taking the time to revise my plan as my thoughts are pleasantly reviewing the year works well. The things I want to keep, as well as those I need to change, are fresh in my mind.

Also, once my plan is set, I can go about enjoying my summer. I can make the most of any shopping excursions, camping trips, and visits to faraway places, picking up a book or activity that will be perfect for a unit I have in mind. The plan isn't set in stone, but it is there, simmering, until it is ready to use. I can't take advantage of these spur-of-the-moment ideas unless I spend some time coming up with my annual plan first, for creating specific center activities is actually the last stage of my planning.

Yearly Planning

We educators have made it a habit of beginning with the specifics. We tried to teach children how to read by teaching isolated sounds, chopping up the context of words and text that might have been comprehended. Young children could sit with a book, grunting and uttering lots of isolated sounds, but too often the connection between these sounds and the words on the page was never made for the child.

We're smarter now, and know how to begin with the whole. We've learned to first show children what reading is all about, and how writing can save our thoughts to remember and reread again and again and again. This is magic to a young child, and what young child can resist magic?

When we begin with specific activities, we wind up with lots of little children running around the classroom, enjoying a wide variety of neat projects. The children are busy, but the connections between an activity and its purpose are not there. Without those connections, no learning takes place. The children have a nice time, but their brains aren't ignited, and so they don't build the understanding that will make them feel how powerful learning can be. There is no magic.

I begin my planning with the total picture for the year: What will I need to teach my students this year? What basic concepts and specific objectives are designated for my students in my school district? These are usually found in your curriculum guides. Pull them out. Take not only the objectives for your year(s), but for the years that come before and after, for every class is filled with children who lag behind in something and those who are zooming full speed ahead. Keep these in the back of your mind as you begin to plan your themes.

Now, think of lots of ideas for thematic units. Brainstorm as many as you can. This step is fun to do with other teachers: more people, more ideas. Put them down randomly; be as general and as specific as you wish. Just get those ideas down on paper.

Start with the concepts required by your district. Think of your textbooks, and what you found interesting in them. Consider trips you will take, your students' backgrounds and interests, and books you have read. Put down concepts taught at your level, such as magnetism, weather, the solar system, animals, plants, the history of your local town, mammals, the environment. You can see already that some of these units will overlap, and some might even overlap with several topics. That's okay. Just have fun and get those ideas down!

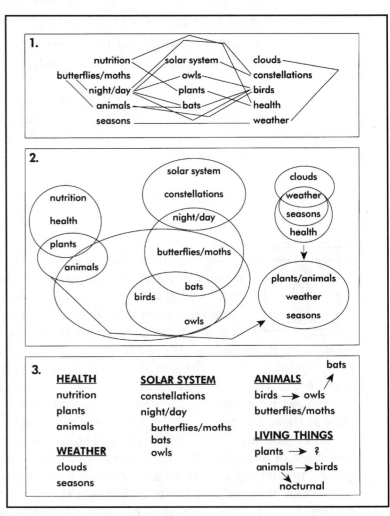

Fig. 4-1 Brainstorming theme ideas

Now you can group these ideas into units. Draw lines connecting any that might go together, or make webs, or create lists — whatever makes sense to you. The idea is to pull them together into groups that have similar concepts. Those that tie into more than one concept should be placed in all that are relevant. For example, let's say you've written nutrition, butterflies and moths, night and day, animals, seasons, the solar system, owls, plants, bats, clouds, constellations, birds, health, and weather. Let's see how we can group them together (see Fig. 4-1).

You can see how they overlap, and how I've come up with some broad themes that might include several mini-units under them. You name each group according to the broad concept, and then you decide which broad concepts you will use during your year. You do not have to decide which specific mini-units you'll bring in, or even in which unit to include them. Your students will determine that, and so your units will change from year to year.

For example, one year you might study owls and bats during the Solar System unit, as your students get interested in nocturnal animals. Another year, you might learn about bats and owls as you study animals, and the children question whether a bat is a bird or not. You might then choose to compare and contrast owls and bats. These specific topics can be organized into the theme that makes connections for your students, and planned at that time. Knowing they are possibilities will allow you to gather some ideas and materials while planning your main thematic units. To help you think of how to create broader topics to use for grouping concepts together thematically, I came up with the chart in Fig. 4-2. These are not complete, and are certainly not set in stone. But they might help you get started planning broader topics, in order to enable your students to make connections in their learning with prior knowledge and experiences they

PLANNING BROAD TOPIC THEMES
Allowing Options and Student Input

ANIMALS:

Birds, Reptiles . . .	Air, Land, Water	Nocturnal
Butterflies & Moths	Habitats	Ocean Life
Farm, Zoo, Pets	Insects & Arachnids	Endangered
Hibernation	Food Chain	Dinosaurs

HEALTH:

Five Senses	Physical Fitness	Plants
Nutrition	All About Me	Reproduction
Drug Prevention	Disease Prevention	New Life

ENVIRONMENT:

Weather	Shadows	Oceans
Seasons	Continents	Collections
Air Pressure	Trees	Natural Resources

COSMOS:

Suns	Moon	Planets
Constellations	Black Holes	Novas

NATURAL HISTORY:

Land Forms	Physical Geography	Fossils
Volcanoes	Rocks & Gems	

PEOPLE:

Personal History	Native Americans	Occupations
Authors & Illustrators	Personal History	Languages
Folktales & Legends	History of Hometown	U.S.A. (States)
Celebrations	Foreign Countries	Immigration

INVENTIONS:

Electricity	Communication	Magnets
Transportation	Simple Machines	

Integrate Thematically Throughout the Year:

Personal Responsibility
caring for others
caring for the planet

Seven Intelligences
artistic expression
creative thinking

Celebrating Diversity
"cultural imagination"
disabilities
storytelling

Curriculum Objectives
language arts
math

Fig. 4-2 Topic themes

bring with them from outside the classroom.

The next step of my planning consists of deciding which broad thematic units I will use, and placing them on the calendar. I like to think of a central focus that my year will take on, and name my units according to that concept. This will allow me to make connections for the children to relate to throughout the entire year. For example, I might focus my year on "The Environment" or "Natural Habitats." (A school I visited recently had chosen "Peace" as its focus for the year. Each thematic unit included activities in peaceful problem solving, emphasizing connections that would encourage this in the children's lives.)

Next I divide my year into main units, where I will focus attention on one area of that main theme (Fig. 4-3). I can then place general concepts and the specific skills that my district has designated for my students under those themes.

The plan I have for next year is included in Fig. 4-4. I want my students to feel they can make a difference in the world, and so I've chosen this as my main concept for the year. The four thematic units will allow me to teach the concepts important to my district, as well as the specific skills my students are ready to learn and will need to know to meet with

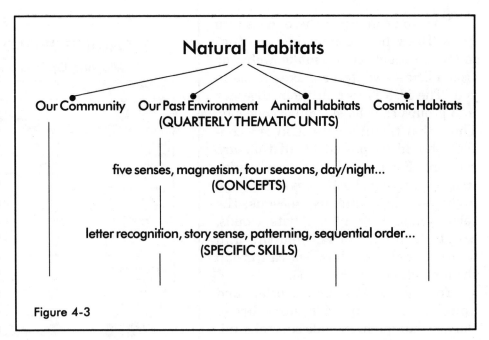

Natural Habitats

Our Community   Our Past Environment   Animal Habitats   Cosmic Habitats
(QUARTERLY THEMATIC UNITS)

five senses, magnetism, four seasons, day/night...
(CONCEPTS)

letter recognition, story sense, patterning, sequential order...
(SPECIFIC SKILLS)

Figure 4-3

success. The concepts will be chosen by what makes sense to use with each theme. The specific skills will go into the units according to the time of year they should be taught as well as the books and activities that I know will encourage the acquisition of those skills.

Now that my year is outlined, I can focus on the activities. Because I began with my goals and planned how I would teach them in a thematic framework, I can plan specific activities for my students that will foster an understanding of concepts and knowledge of specific skills. They will learn from interacting with the materials I choose because they will be able to make the connections between what they are doing and how it relates to the lessons I am teaching. They will learn general concepts and use information in meaningful experiences, and they will understand. That information will belong to them, for they have spent time applying what they know.

That's the magic of center time. But as you can see, there must be a firm foundation laid before the games and activities ever enter the room. Without the planning, it's just a lot of stuff. Without the planning, the children will work with the materials, but the connections won't be there, and soon, the activity will become off-task, for there will be no

intrinsic motivation to learn and understand.

When this planning is done as a group, it is even better to begin early. If several teachers are working together as a team, school monies might be used to order specific materials to be used in the units. You might choose to create files for each unit, and keep ideas for trade books and interesting activities that you come across in the files, so that they are ready to pull together as you begin to plan the unit in detail. School librarians can also be advised of the units in order to locate resource books that could be included in their ordering. This is particularly important if several classrooms or grade levels will use the same materials. The librarian might wish to focus book displays and pull small collections to be set out for your students.

Student Involvement in Planning

As I have mentioned, planning general topics allows you the flexibility to include your students in the planning. They can suggest specific topics within each unit for further investigation. For example, in the thematic plan shown in Fig. 4-3, students might suggest a mini-unit on endangered animals during the study of animal habitats. You can incorporate

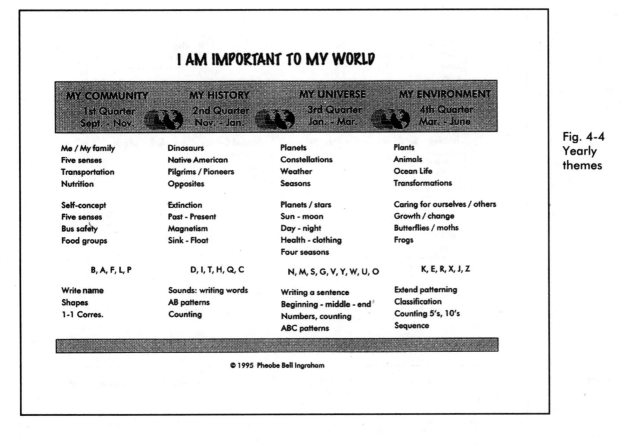

I AM IMPORTANT TO MY WORLD

MY COMMUNITY 1st Quarter Sept. - Nov.	MY HISTORY 2nd Quarter Nov. - Jan.	MY UNIVERSE 3rd Quarter Jan. - Mar.	MY ENVIRONMENT 4th Quarter Mar. - June
Me / My family	Dinosaurs	Planets	Plants
Five senses	Native American	Constellations	Animals
Transportation	Pilgrims / Pioneers	Weather	Ocean Life
Nutrition	Opposites	Seasons	Transformations
Self-concept	Extinction	Planets / stars	Caring for ourselves / others
Five senses	Past - Present	Sun - moon	Growth / change
Bus safety	Magnetism	Day - night	Butterflies / moths
Food groups	Sink - Float	Health - clothing	Frogs
		Four seasons	
B, A, F, L, P	D, I, T, H, Q, C	N, M, S, G, V, Y, W, U, O	K, E, R, X, J, Z
Write name	Sounds: writing words	Writing a sentence	Extend patterning
Shapes	AB patterns	Beginning - middle - end	Classification
1-1 Corres.	Counting	Numbers, counting	Counting 5's, 10's
		ABC patterns	Sequence

© 1995 Pheobe Bell Ingraham

Fig. 4-4
Yearly
themes

this topic into the goals you have already set for this unit.

While you can plan mini-units in response to a widespread interest of one class, it is impossible and unnecessary to plan individual thematic units for each child in your class. When only one or a few students are interested in a precise topic, you might suggest they design an individual study unit (discussed in Chapter 8) on that area. This will let your students feel empowered in their learning and encourage them to take responsibility for it.

When planning activities for each thematic unit, be sure to include a wide variety of experiences specific to your students, their community, as well as special events occurring during this unit, field trips, music, art, drama, and food experiences. There are many ways to ensure that you include all subject areas, as well as "extra" experiences, events, and activities. Traditional webs for planning individual thematic units (see Fig. 4-5; reproducible on page 170) may be used, or you may wish to plan around your centers.

To ensure that you have integrated your unit into all areas of your curriculum, use your contract or center chart (Fig. 4-6; reproducible on page 171), and list at least three activities in each area that will make a connection to the thematic topic. You might also choose to incorporate the seven intelligences within your planning (Fig. 4-7), to ensure that the abilities of all your students are nurtured in the investigation into this topic.

The activities found in each center should be created around activities that the children associate with the theme. Do not try to stretch too far, just to include a food experience or a favorite project. If the activities do not flow naturally from the concepts, your students will not see the connections and their work with them will not be meaningful or have any real purpose. Their work in that center will become thoughtless and off-task.

For example, when studying health and

Fig. 4-5
Try using thematic webbing to plan your activities . . .

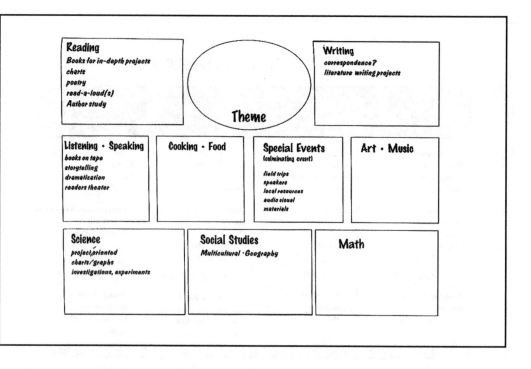

Reading
Books for in-depth projects
charts
poetry
read-a-loud(s)
Author study

Theme

Writing
correspondence?
literature writing projects

Listening · Speaking
books on tape
storytelling
dramatization
readers theater

Cooking · Food

Special Events
(culminating event)
field trips
speakers
local resources
audio visual
materials

Art · Music

Science
project oriented
charts/graphs
investigations, experiments

Social Studies
Multicultural · Geography

Math

Fig. 4-6
. . . or plan around your centers using your contract or center chart.

Whales: Zoobooks
A House for Hermit Crab — Golden
The Little Island - MacDonald
Sam, Bangs {Moonshine — Evaline Ness
Fish Eyes — Lois Ehlert
Swimmy - Leo Lionni

Australia — Great Barrier Reef
Mem Fox author study

Shells — count, class, pattern, add, subt.

Fish Crackers — add/subt. mult./divide

"Stuffed" fish
Color - blue "wash"
diorama

ABC Book - Jerry Palotta

House/Hermit Crab (mural)
Write Story...
A Beach Day - Douglas Florian
Postcards!

Response Log

hermit Crabs
Shells - classify, weigh,graph mag. glass
make an ocean jar

paint beach scene- glue sand

library   language   writing   journal
math   geography   science   easel
art   role play   blocks   games

beach
Store: souvenirs Swim/beach items

sandbox
molds

Also: Speakers, Trips, Music, Food/cooking

Activities for Each Center for Thematic Unit: Oceans

nutrition, it would be a natural extension to operate a small restaurant, designing menus that would include foods they could easily prepare and serve in your classroom (Fig. 4-8). For a kindergarten or primary classroom, the children would focus only on the behavior necessary for ordering, making, and serving the food. For older children, the use of money might be included, and the students might find it necessary to count change and balance the books at the end of each day.

Asking students to complete a worksheet about a balanced diet in the restaurant would not be a natural extension of that area. It would, in fact, detract from the meaningful, purposeful play that the children engage

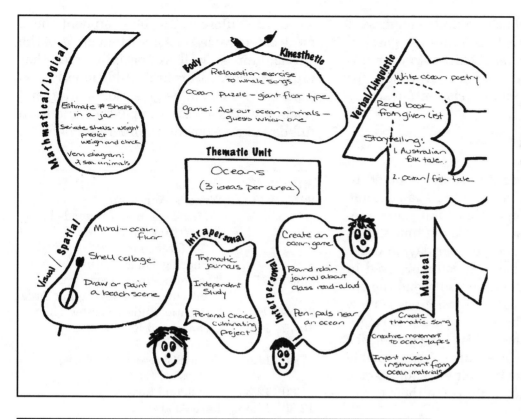

Fig. 4-7 Planning themes and activities around multiple intelligences theory is also a good approach.

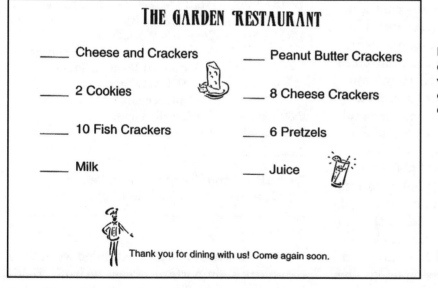

Fig. 4-8 Creating a sample menu and running a small restaurant would be appropriate learning center activities for children who are studying a unit on nutrition.

in, and should not be included in this area.

However, students might be asked before opening the restaurant to design a menu around the food groups, offering food items for each. Publishing a cookbook of favorite family recipes is also an appropriate project for this unit; however, it should be placed in a research or publishing center, rather than a dramatic play area.

Again, the task should be placed in a center where the activity is naturally part of your students' activities, or it will detract from the purpose of both the task and the center.

Learning through play does not mean that making connections becomes haphazard or merely by chance. The teacher must know his students well, and design activities that are interesting to them, while engaging them in activities that establish an understanding of the skills and concepts that are the goals of the unit. It is important to listen to your students and allow them to offer suggestions for activities that you can develop into learning tasks.

Center Time in Your Daily Routine

Once your students are accustomed to working in centers, your schedule can become more fixed, with center time taking up a predictable segment each day. Center time should last at least 45–50 minutes per day, in order to give students time to become involved in their work. Some children will spend the entire time involved in the work of one center, but most will work in two centers during a one-hour center time. This is important, for the choices the children are making enable them to get involved in their work and decide where and how they will extend their learning for that day.

When we are involved in many center activities in the middle of a thematic unit, I like to give one day per week to a longer center time. In this way, I encourage the children to become immersed in the work they enjoy. They can work uninterrupted on projects they have become involved in, and I can have additional opportunities to conference and work with small groups.

In a half-day kindergarten, I place center time in the middle of our three-hour session. The first hour can be given to journaling time, total group lessons in literacy and math, and mini-lessons on new tasks in centers. No task goes out in my centers until I have given instructions on how it should be completed. The last hour can be devoted to music, stories, playground time, and general review of the learning that happened in the centers.

Think of the day in thirds: the first portion introduces information and skills in order to proceed in centers; the second portion is center time; the third portion summarizes or celebrates what has taken place in center time, through stories, songs, poetry, or sharing of work.

For full-day programs, the breakdown is somewhat different. The older students have more extensive lessons in certain areas of the curriculum, as well as special classes that must be worked around. Additionally, extended time should be given for writing and reading workshops. A sample schedule for a full day in an elementary program might be:

8:15 - 8:30	Opening
8:30 - 9:30	Writer's Workshop
	Mini-Lesson and Extended Writing Time
	Conferencing
	Sharing Their Writing
9:30 - 9:45	Thematic Mini-Lesson
	Introduction of New Center Tasks
9:45 - 10:45	Thematic Studies: Center Time
10:45 - 11:00	Cleanup and Review of Center Work
11:00 - 11:30	Special Classes (Art, Music, Physical Ed.)
11:30 - 12:30	Lunch and Recess
12:30 - 12:45	Read Aloud
12:45 - 1:30	Math: Lesson and *Math Their Way* Activities
1:30 - 2:30	Reader's Workshop
	Mini-Lesson/Shared Reading
	Extended Reading Time (DEAR/SSR)*
	Conferencing
2:30 - 2:45	Book Talk Time
2:45 - 2:50	Cleanup and Dismissal

* DEAR = Drop Everything And Read/
SSR = Silent Sustained Reading

In this schedule, I give extended work time to my most important areas: writing, reading, and math. These segments allow for direct instruction and time for each student to practice their skills in this specific area. My center time comes in the middle of the morning, when the children are becoming fidgety and need to move about. They have spent extended time writing, and now can listen to a short lesson introducing new center tasks or hear a story that gives insight into our thematic unit. The afternoon is spent with more direct instruction of the specific skills they will need in order to feel competent in their individual work, with time given for individual practice and ongoing assessment.

The skills the children learn support and extend their work in center activities. The center activities take the specific skills they have learned and utilize them in the content areas. Each portion of our day supports the independent learning we do in our center time, bringing meaning and focus to the development of skills important to each age/grade level.

You must adapt your schedule to your own school day, your special classes, and your needs. Remember to balance total group lessons with busy work sessions. List your priorities and give the most important areas the most time. But above all else, allow for extended time for children to be engaged in learning. That means they are spending time doing, without interruption, whatever it is you expect them to learn.

Weekly and Daily Planning

Lesson plans for classrooms designed around centers will look somewhat different than those of a traditional classroom. Centers to be utilized might be described on index cards (Fig. 4-9), with specific activities and their curricular goals listed. Then these are simply plotted onto daily lesson plans in order to keep track of what has been introduced, and what groups have completed which activities.

Detailed lesson plans will be frustrating to attempt, for centers must be maintained with flexibility. Your time is better spent planning for the unit, making certain it is of interest to the children in your classroom, and that it meets their specific needs as well as the district guidelines for your curriculum.

I have used a traditional plan book, but rather than block out the centers on a daily basis, I've included a center column in my book that goes along the week, rather than corresponding to the day (Fig. 4-10). In that way, I can use plan books from previous years to recall when an activity was introduced and what literature I used in order to introduce new tasks. I can recall what tasks I placed in each center as I went through a thematic unit. I do not always include all the generic materials in those centers in my lesson plans, for they are usually there throughout the year once introduced. I list only tasks specific to that thematic unit, and those generic jobs that I wish to emphasize or check the students' ability to accomplish (see the center column of the plan book shown in Fig. 4-10).

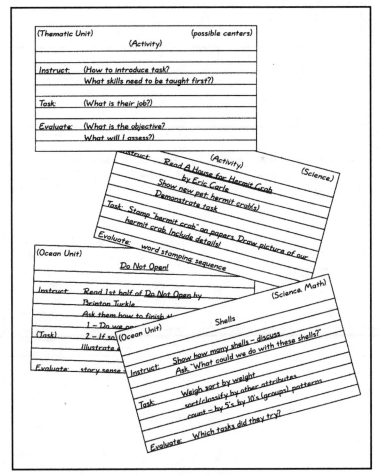

Fig. 4-9 Creating learning center activities on individual index cards lets you sort and re-sort to come up with different combinations for your learning centers.

Fig. 4-10

LESSON PLANS Week Beginning January 23, 1995 — Teacher

	Opening	Lang. Arts / Develop.	Curriculum Develop.	Music / Movement
MONDAY 23	Fab. Friend / Attendance Pledge / News / January G. Between W. / # Stars!	Intro Mm / Sound objects / Writing / Tasks / Handsign / Mother! Mother!	Science / Rainbow Book of Facts About Space	January / Songs and fingerplays
TUESDAY 24	Surprise Box / Attendance Pledge / News / Journals / Book Look	Literature Link ~ / Mother, Mother, I Want Another!	Math / Review Shapes	
WEDNESDAY 25	Favorite Book	Mm picture sharing	Geography / Antarctica ~ / Plan a Flag	
THURSDAY 26	Choose Songs	Tactile ABC: / Mm is for macaroni / Norton/Gellian/parent / Hagen volunteers	Science / Space game for Games Center	Children's Choice!
FRIDAY 27		Taste Mm / Macaroni and cheese	Writing / Goodnight Moon / books	

LESSON PLANS Week Beginning _____ 19____ — Teacher

	Center Activities	Center (PPAs) Objectives	Story	Gross Motor
MONDAY	Language - Mm jobs / ABC puzzles / Name game / ABC Word Book / Writing / The Mitten Song / Writing names		Goodnight Moon / (Big Book)	Outside / When possible / Inside / when wet/cold
TUESDAY	Library - Jan. book / chart - mitten Song / tape - one Light, / one Sun / ABC words, mag. / Art / Snowy Day / pictures		M and M counting book	
WEDNESDAY	Easel - paint on blue / snowmen / Games - maze, colors, / puzzles, space / game / Role Play / house! (change places)		Fab. Friends favorite book	
THURSDAY	Science / Solar System / moon, stars, sun / Geography / Antarctica / books / flags (penguins)		Record - Rainbow / Book of Facts: / Space	
FRIDAY	Math - / shapes / patterns (and) / counting / Blocks - / building / Build Books		Happy, Birthday, Moon	

Fig. 4-10 The center column in this plan book helps me see how my learning center activities tie into other aspects of my thematically oriented instruction.

Fig. 4-11

Ingraham Kindergarten — EDK   Date _____   Week # _____   Fabulous Friend: _____   Birthdays: _____

	Opening Circle — Journals	Language Arts	Curriculum Development	Center Activities — Objectives	Closing Circle Time	F. Direct / Listening	Language Experience	Curriculum Reinforcement
Monday	Attendance Pledge — News / Calendar Math / Journals / Book Look			Language / Writing / Journals	Music / Story	Exercise Video / Poetry Reading		
Tuesday	Attendance Pledge — News / Calendar Math / Journals / Book Look			Library / Role Play	Music / Story	Exercise Video / Poetry Reading		
Wednesday	Attendance Pledge — News / Calendar Math / Journals / Book Look			Math / Science	Music / Story	Exercise Video / Poetry Reading		
Thursday	Attendance Pledge — News / Calendar Math / Journals / Book Look			Geography / Art	Music / Story	Exercise Video / Poetry Reading		
Friday	Attendance Pledge — News / Calendar Math / Journals / Book Look			Easel / Games / Blocks	Music / Story	Exercise Video / Poetry Reading		

Fig. 4-11 I created this form on my computer using WordPerfect 5.2 for Windows.

If your school allows you to use your own lesson plan style, a three-ring binder works well. It can hold copies of weekly lesson plans created on the computer along with ideas for activities, assessment and anecdotal record sheets, checklists on who has accomplished what tasks, pages with pockets for index cards, copies of songs or poetry you wish to include, letters and calendars sent home to parents, and booklists appropriate for that unit (see Fig. 4-11). This is my favorite way to organize my thematic unit ideas, lesson plans, and center activities in one central location.

If you prefer a bound plan book, there are several suitable to use for this type of planning. A few are listed at the end of the chapter.

Lesson Plans and Substitutes

Running your classroom like this takes time and patience, and when you run out of steam or decide to get some additional skills by attending a workshop, how do you tell a substitute teacher how to do this? The best possible way to inform your substitutes is to have your principal invite them to school for an observation day. Let them see it all in action. They will be better prepared to conduct a meaningful day for your students in your absence.

But lesson plans for a sub can be overwhelming in this type of structure. I finally came up with a form that I use, and every substitute I have had in my classroom has appreciated it.

On my computer, I type out my daily agenda with possible descriptions of each area of activity included (see Fig. 4-12). I also leave space in each area to write the specific activity that I would like the sub to complete during this time. In this way, the teacher has

Extended Day Kindergarten Schedule

8:10 - 8:45	Opening Circle and Journaling Attendance, Pledge, News Calendar Math Journals: mini-lessons and sharing Book Look (SSR)
8:45 - 9:00	Language Arts Shared Reading Letter Study / Phonetic Skills
9:00 - 9:20	Curriculum Development Integrated Thematic Instruction Task Introduction
9:20 - 10:25	Center Time Independent Practice Time Individual Instruction and Evaluation
10:25 - 10:45	Closing Circle Time Music, fingerplays, and games Story: Read Aloud Ready to go: check cubbies, get coats
10:45 - 11:00	Outside Play: Gross Motor Development Dismissal: Morning Children
11:00 - 12:30	Lunch, Playground, and Rest
12:30 - 1:00	Listening Activities Exercise Video, Following Directions, Listening Games Poetry, Repeated Reading Activities
1:00 - 1:30	Language Lab - computer time
1:30 - 2:15	Curriculum Reinforcement Alphabet Journals, Letter Games Math Their Way Lessons and Tubbing Small Group Activities
2:15 - 2:20 2:20 - 2:55	Clean Up - Dismissal of Early Bus Students Enrichment Activities for Small Group Shared Reading, Children's Choice Story Language Experience Chart Gross Motor: Outside Play
2:55 - 3:00	Ready to Go: Dismissal Out at Bus

Fig. 4-12 This daily agenda form gives substitute teachers a detailed view of what goes on during the day in my classroom.

an idea of how the whole day will run, sees what else we do at this time each day, and knows just what to do with the children within the context of her usual time with me (see Fig. 4-13). I usually write my specific information with a red pen so that it stands out. These are not only very helpful for someone new to your classroom, but they are much easier for you to prepare. Each time you are out, you do not have to re-explain what you mean by "Center Time" or "Curriculum Development Time." You simply write in what should be taught during this time today.

Along with these lesson plans I have a Substitutes' Notebook with more detailed descriptions of my centers, my rules, departure notes on students, attendance sheets, and any other information about my classroom

Extended Day Kindergarten Schedule

Time	Activity	Notes (handwritten)
8:10 - 8:45	**Opening Circle and Journaling** Attendance, Pledge, News Calendar (Math) Journals: mini-lessons and sharing Book Look (SSR)	What did they like best for 100 Day? letters → words → sentences → story
8:45 - 9:00	**Language Arts** Shared Reading Letter Study / Phonetic Skills	Valentine Interactive Chart Take turns having the children point - everyone reads
9:00 - 9:20	**Curriculum Development** Integrated Thematic Instruction Task Introduction	Goodnight Moon books: 1. make covers 2. cut their completed pages
9:20 - 10:25	**Center Time** Independent Practice Time Individual Instruction and Evaluation (* computer group at 10:00)	* children with completed Valentines should go to Role Play - Post office.
10:25 - 10:45	**Closing Circle Time** Music, fingerplays, and games Story: Read Aloud Ready to go: check cubbies, get coats	Val. chart sung to tune of "Skip to My Lou" Moongame by Frank Asch
10:45 - 11:00	**Outside Play: Gross Motor Development** Dismissal: Morning Children	
11:00 - 12:30	**Lunch, Playground, and Rest**	
12:30 - 1:00	**Listening Activities** Exercise Video Following Directions, Listening Games (tv in closet) Poetry, Repeated Reading Activities	The Jigaree
1:00 - 1:30	**Language Lab - computer time**	
1:30 - 2:15	**Curriculum Reinforcement** Alphabet Journals, Letter Games Math Their Way Lessons and Tubbing Small Group Activities	Complete one page of their own Jigaree book (pages on my desk)
2:15 - 2:20	**Clean Up - Dismissal of Early Bus Students**	
2:20 - 2:55	**Enrichment Activities for Small Group** Shared Reading, Children's Choice Story Language Experience Chart Gross Motor: Outside Play	Choose 1 center Then Book Look or a Story chosen by them.
2:55 - 3:00	**Ready to Go: Dismissal Out at Bus**	

Fig. 4-13 Adding details about activities planned for a specific day makes it easy for the substitute to manage the classroom and keep the children on-task in my absence.

that my substitute teachers need. They can refer to this when they have a question or a free moment, but the lesson plans are there to get them started immediately with the children.

Teaching a Concept and Introducing New Tasks

I rarely place materials out into my centers until I have introduced them, showing the children how they are to be used. The only exception I can think of is in math, where we have free exploration during tubbing or in our math center. Even then, I show the children how to take care of the materials, even though I am not telling them directly what it is they should do with them. ("Free exploration" and "tubbing" are terms used in *Math Their Way*. It is an excellent program built upon a very

child-centered, developmentally appropriate philosophy. I highly recommend it.)

Every morning, I begin the day with journal writing. This block of time often includes a mini-lesson and sharing of our journals. Each day also includes a math lesson with my calendar, and a language lesson that teaches some area of my language arts curriculum. It usually involves shared reading, poetry, letters and sounds, and/or reading aloud.

For different age levels, you would look at your objectives and prioritize them, coming up with the activities you will include as separate blocks of time. For me, these are writer's workshop, a math mini-lesson, and independent reading (SSR — Silent Sustained Reading, or DEAR — Drop Everything And Read) time. My other total group instruction is titled "Curriculum Development

Here I model the bean bag toss activity for my students during circle time.

I monitor my centers closely. I watch to see how the children are working with the materials. I keep track of who has practiced what and who still needs to complete a task. I have found that when I've introduced a task well, it is completed with great care. When I teach a new skill, and place a job in the centers that will enable the children to practice that skill, they are usually eager to do their best. If they aren't, I reteach it, because I probably messed it up.

I also watch to see when behaviors change. When children have used materials appropriately, and suddenly their behavior changes and they begin to "abuse" it, rather than use it, I know it's time to remove that job and put a new one in its place.

For example, when I introduce a new concept in science, I often put several tasks out to reinforce what I've taught. I might do this over a period of two to three days, depending upon how many activities I'm putting out, and what needs to be taught before the children can work independently at that center.

Let's say we're learning about magnets. I might place magnetic marbles, a magnetic maze, a game where you use a magnet to place

Time." During this part of my day, I introduce new concepts and specific skills, open new centers, and introduce new tasks to my students.

I have several standard plans for accomplishing this. I often use a trade book to begin a new unit or teach a concept. I usually use poetry or a Big Book with a shared reading activity for a specific language skill. If the task is to be in the art or science area, I often model the behavior I want to see.

Sometimes, I model the task in complete silence. The children have to watch very closely if I'm not narrating my actions! After I am through, I ask them to tell me what I did. I think this is my favorite method, other than using my favorite trade books. I just love that silence.

Often, I begin by asking the children what they think I should do with the materials I lay before them. When they tell me what to do, not only do they tend to remember it better, but they often come up with a neat idea I'd not thought of or a better way of accomplishing it! Once the concept is clear and the directions are understood, we put the new task out in the center.

Later, the bean bag toss activity is placed in the gross motor/ block center.

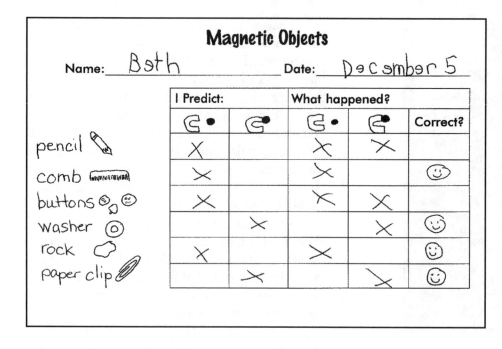

Magnetic Objects

Name: Bəth   Date: Dəcəmbər 5

	I Predict:		What happened?		Correct?
pencil	X		X	X	
comb	X		X		☺
buttons	X		X	X	
washer		X		X	☺
rock	X		X		☺
paper clip		X		X	☺

Fig 4-14 Here, a kindergartner predicted whether or not each object was magnetic, then tested her predictions and recorded her result.

colored dots on a grid forming a picture or design, and a variety of magnets to experiment with. I will also introduce a new task that everyone must do. Here, it might be a bowl of objects, a magnet, and a board divided in half: One side shows an object sticking to a magnet, the other shows a magnet and an object that are not touching. The children must predict if each object will stick to the magnet or not. I will also place a form (Fig. 4-14; reproducible on page 172) and some pencils in the science center so that they can record their predictions and the results.

This is a task they must do when they come to science. The other magnet jobs are there for them to try, but the prediction chart is a *must-do* task. They cannot leave the center until that job is completed. Some of their must-do jobs can be taken home as soon as I've seen them and recorded that they have accomplished the task. Others must be saved and examined in more detail, so that I can take notations about their progress. These go in the completed work basket in the middle of my room.

After a few weeks, I may notice that the children are misusing the magnetic marbles. I know that it is time to remove these from the center and replace them with a new job.

In this way, materials are constantly going in and out of my centers without my having to change the center completely. It also keeps me from having to give too many instructions all in one day.

Additionally, when each child has completed the magnetic prediction sheet, we discuss the results in our group meeting, and a new task is introduced that the children must accomplish when they visit the science center. Again, this is the way new materials move in and out of my centers. I have found this works best for me, so that I am not at school changing my room completely around every few weeks. I've also found that when I tried introducing all the new center jobs every Monday, it became frustrating for the children to sit so long, and they did not remember how to do anything. It was way too much at one time. Giving instructions for one new area per day has proven to be more efficient and effective.

Creating Center Activities

I design the activities for my students with several things in mind. I do not like frivolous projects, done with no real reason for their completion. One of the dangers with center activities is that the "fun" aspect takes on

A Winter Poem

SanTa
REINdeer
SLA
SNoWm an
ice
SNoW

ZAC

by _____

Fig 4-15 A "list" poem based on a mini-lesson on inventive spelling

greater importance than the reasons for accomplishing the task. When this happens, your room gets filled with a lot of fun and games, the children soon lose control, and the learning gets lost in the process.

Everything I ask my children to do has a purpose. They do not always understand all the objectives I have in mind, but they see a purpose for their work.

There are just a few priorities I keep in mind as I plan my center tasks. Here are the ones I feel are most important:

1. I like activities that allow each child to think creatively. This means that they must be somewhat open-ended. My bulletin boards do not display 25 identical projects, colored in the same way with the same colors used for each section. If we made penguins, we would have a board filled with 25 different penguin species, each one subtly different than the last.

2. I like activities that give my students opportunities to practice specific skills in the context of some greater work. For example, my class this year particularly loves to hear poetry, so I decided to help them write their

own poems. We began with some very simple "list" poems (see Figure 4-15), completed after a mini-lesson on invented spelling strategies (otherwise known as a phonics lesson). I did not want them to have to sound out too many words, but I did want to give them several opportunities to try different words. The children used a combination of inventive spellings ("sla") and familiar words ("white"), and words found on charts or books around the room ("reindeer"). Combining the phonetic skill lesson with the joy of poetry proved to be a perfect match for this group. I had to create several different sheets for them to place in our writing center, for they continued to ask to write more poems for weeks.

You never know what will happen when you use a creative activity to mask dull chores. One day I was giving Brittany an individualized lesson on vocabulary development and the use of the picture dictionary. Remembering her love for the poetry activity, she used that format to create a poem from new words she found in our dictionary (see Fig. 4-16). Brittany learned more than vocabulary and dictionary skills: Brittany learned how to learn!

3. Whenever possible, I try to link a new task with the current thematic unit. For example, we can create patterns the entire year, yet the job would be different each time, as the pattern changes (making the task more difficult) and the materials to pattern change with the theme. I cannot always make the task specific to the unit, but I try.

4. I like to include writing whenever possible. Even if they are just writing one word, my students need to feel the power literacy brings to their lives. Whenever they write, I know they'll have lots of chances to re-read what they've written, and the best way to build reading skills is to read, read, READ!

Fig 4-16 This student chose to create a list poem using her newfound dictionary skills

Resources

Caine, Renate Nummela, and Caine, Geoffrey. *Teaching and the Human Brain*. Alexandria, VA: Association for Supervision and Curriculum Development, 1991.

Campbell, Bruce. *The Multiple Intelligences Handbook: Lesson Plans and More . . .* Stanwood, WA: Campbell & Associates, 1994.

Davies, Anne, and Politano, Colleen. *Making Themes Work*. Winnipeg: Peguis, 1993.

Faculty of the New City School. *Celebrating Multiple Intelligences: Teaching for Success*. St. Louis, MO: The New City School, Inc., 1994.

Lazear, David. *Seven Ways of Knowing: Teaching for Multiple Intelligences*. Palatine, IL: Skylight Publishing, 1991.

————. *Seven Ways of Teaching: The Artistry of Teaching With Multiple Intelligences*. Palatine, IL: Skylight Publishing, 1991.

Lesson Plan Books

The Complete Lesson Plan Book
ISBN 0-9627389-5-6; and

The Multiyear Lesson Plan Book
(includes room for two years of planning)
ISBN 1-884548-10-5; both from

Crystal Springs Books
Ten Sharon Road
PO Box 500
Peterborough, NH 03458
1-800-321-0401

Lesson Plan Book and Lesson Plan Book II
(CTP 3321 and CTP 3326)
Creative Teaching Press
PO Box 6017
Cypress, CA 90630-0017
1-800-444-4287

Chapter 5

Assessment and Evaluation

In Piaget's view, developmental assessment is a continual process that records the actual work children do during the year. A collection of the child's work, a folder containing some of her writing, some of his work in math, and science, etc., is much more meaningful than a grade. Keeping such a record, and making decisions about what samples of work are to be contained in it, is a valuable learning experience in itself. The same cannot be said for taking tests. In short, documentation rather than examination is consistent with the educational philosophy of the active classroom.

—David Elkind, *Child Development and Education: A Piagetian Perspective*

One question I'm asked often during my presentations is how I ensure that everyone stays on-task, completing each assignment or activity correctly. I feel responsible for ensuring that each child is exposed to the appropriate curriculum. I do this through direct instruction of the total group, small groups, and individuals. I work to encourage personal responsibility and intrinsic motivation.

I realize that I cannot always determine what activity is "off-task" for my students; conversation is a useful part of the learning process. I teach my students how to work in this environment, and then spend my time in class encouraging the learning process.

Much of the assessment and evaluation that I do is done in class during center time, as I move from child to child, taking anecdotal notes about their work, listening to them read, or asking them to explain their work to me. In this manner, I am able to take advantage of those "teachable moments" when

I see that a child is ready for a lesson in a particular area. For example, the child who is writing word lists about a drawing can be shown how to use those words in a sentence to tell me a story about her picture. I am also able to reteach a skill when I observe a child incorrectly completing a task, such as patterning or writing letters.

I also assess progress through documentation of the children's completed work. Keeping track of which center each child has worked in allows me to know quickly how the children are moving through their week, and what tasks they have accomplished that they can take home immediately. I often evaluate their journals as well as other work that is done "on paper" after they leave. I keep track of their work and their progress, just as any other teacher does.

I give individual or small group assessments to keep track in a more standardized way of the progress the children are making. Combining all of these methods allows me to know that each child is progressing as an individual, from the point at which he began his year, while also making certain he is staying on target according to his age-appropriate guidelines.

These assessments help me keep a close eye on children who might need additional help or a different teaching approach. I am always considering both aspects (individually

appropriate and age-appropriate) of developmentally appropriate instruction so that I am assured no child slips between the cracks.

Evaluation and assessment are integrated into my day just as learning specific skills is integrated into the context of our classroom activities. It is difficult for me to discuss my teaching without mentioning evaluation, for the two are intertwined in a series of actions and reactions. I know what to teach and what activities to place in my centers because my assessments show that the children are ready for, or in need of, certain experiences.

When you ignore evaluation as part of your daily routine in center time, you run the risk of stagnation in student achievement. Constant focus on what the child is doing and how she goes about her work allows you to know when to give those "gentle nudges" (as Donald Graves refers to them) that encourage growth and progress.

In this chapter, I will explain what I do in my classroom that keeps me informed of my students' work.

Ongoing Evaluation of Student Work

The most obvious way I keep track of the children's work on an individual basis is through their center charts. I make a quick check of their completed work as they change centers; that way, I know that they have completed the task there. Some of their projects (in all centers) need to go home immediately, for they are anxious to share it with their families. This is good, for they are reinforcing their learning when they explain it at home.

Not all tasks need microscopic evaluation. For example, when the children complete a science paper showing what objects sink and which ones float, they can take it home that day. Or when they complete a flag in the geography center, I do not always need to check to see how it was done.

I often keep a class roster at centers to cross out the name of each child as she completes the work there. This helps especially when projects go on longer than a week.

Informal assessment can take place as I listen to a child read something he has written.

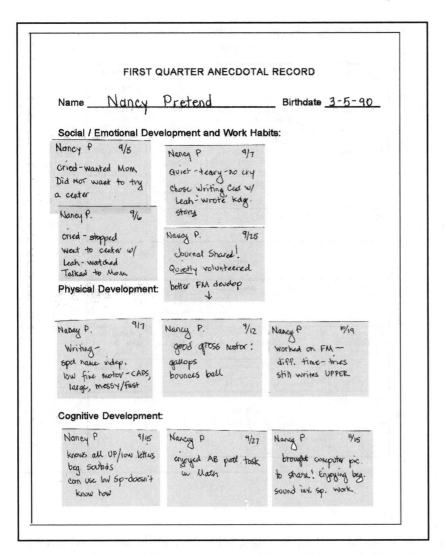

FIRST QUARTER ANECDOTAL RECORD

Name __Nancy Pretend__ Birthdate __3-5-90__

Social / Emotional Development and Work Habits:

> Nancy P   9/5
> Cried - wanted Mom
> Did not want to try
> a center

> Nancy P   9/7
> Quiet - teary - no cry
> Chose writing cnt w/
> Leah - wrote kdg.
> story

> Nancy P.   9/6
> cried - stopped
> went to center w/
> Leah - watched
> Talked to Mom

> Nancy P.   9/25
> Journal Shared!
> Quietly volunteered
> better FM develop
> ↓

Physical Development:

> Nancy P.   9/7
> Writing -
> spd name indep.
> low fine motor - CAPS,
> large, messy/fast

> Nancy P.   9/12
> good gross motor:
> gallops
> bounces ball

> Nancy P   10/19
> worked on FM -
> diff. time - tries
> still writes UPPER

Cognitive Development:

> Nancy P   9/15
> knows all UP/low letters
> beg. sounds
> can use Inv Sp - doesn't
> know how

> Nancy P   9/27
> enjoyed AB patt. task
> in Math

> Nancy P   11/15
> brought computer pic.
> to share! Enjoying beg.
> sound inv. sp. work.

Fig. 5-1 I write my observations of children on Post-it™ notes, then stick them to each child's anecdotal record. The information I gather goes beyond skills assessment to include behavior, moods, and social interaction. It's a good idea, once the Post-it™ notes are organized, to transfer the information permanently to the form.

Keeping individual anecdotal records on children's work is very helpful as I review their progress and decide what tasks or skills they need to be learning. These are done in a variety of ways. As I move about the room during center time, I will watch a child complete a task. I jot down my observations onto small Post-it™ notes, including the child's name and the date. These notes are later placed on an Anecdotal Record Form in my notebook, like the one in Fig. 5-1; (reproducible on page 173). I report only what the child is doing, without trying to evaluate or interpret the child's actions. When these notes are compiled, they give me indications about what I need to emphasize with that child.

When a child rereads his writing, calls me over to hear him read a chart, or brings me a book that he retells, I jot down what he did, and post that note on his anecdotal sheet. After reteaching a child to make an A-B pattern, I document the lesson and place it on his form. By the end of the quarter, I have a real sense of the way the child learns and the progress he's made, simply by reading and comparing the notations about his work.

Writing the notes doesn't take much time, but it does take discipline to remember to do them consistently. A good time to take notes is during the last ten minutes of center time, once you've announced that there will be no more center changes. The children will be busy completing their work, and you will not be distracted by marking charts. I have found this the best time to make a habit of anecdotal notations.

I have also used a calendar form for keeping anecdotal records (see Fig. 5-2; repro-

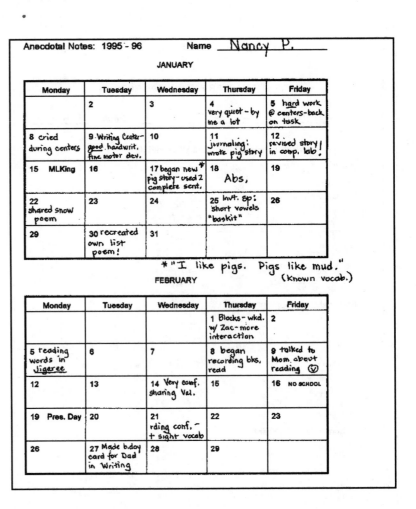

Fig. 5-2 This month-by-month anecdotal calendar makes it easy to see the "big picture" in terms of the child's development, as well as patterns of emotional ups and downs and absences.

ducible on page 174). I can put four months onto one sheet (by using both sides of the paper), and keep the sheets in my lesson plan notebook so they are always on hand in my classroom. I sometimes jot down something quickly right on the spot, if I want to remember the child's exact words, or I can sit at the end of center time and recall work each child was doing.

I have found that this format works very well, for I can more easily get a picture of each child's development at a glance. I can also keep notations I need to recall for each child. For example, when worried that a child is missing too much school, I can begin to write his absences in red on his anecdotal calendar. In this format, it is easy to see any patterns to his absences. I can also jot down when I have called a parent for a conference or sent a note home with a child.

The first page of this calendar includes a beginning-of-the-year child profile which has information on the child's development in several important areas (see Fig. 5-3).

Documentation and Evaluation

Keeping track of children's individual progress through documentation of their work is managed through our portfolios. Portfolio assessment can be accomplished in some form with even young children. While their reflections on their work are not as polished or detailed as with older students, they can be taught the concept of reviewing their work to gain insight into how they are changing and growing. They can make observations about projects, reflecting on the way they worked at a task, or how much they learned about something when we had "that task" in the science center.

For example, my students each make a tactile alphabet book. It takes most of the year

Anecdotal Notes: __94-95__   Name __Beth__

Child Profile: Beginning of the Year

Fine Motor: __good__   Behavior: __good - responds to me__
Listening: __loves books/social__   Reading Stage: __beg → fluent__
Speech/Oral Lang: __✓ good vocab.__   Writing Stage: __early fluency__
__Beth loves to write - rereads own writing well.__
__Inv. Spelling errors - reading accuracy Early with__
__good comprehension but lots of errors__

AUGUST

Monday	Tuesday	Wednesday	Thursday	Friday
		23 Journals - lots of Inv Sp! Gd. story sense	24 Library - read to me - accuracy + comp.	25 Lots of talk during Tot Grp. quieted
28 Math Cent - bossing boys	29 Good listening gd. centers			

Fig. 5-3 The first page of the calendar includes a beginning-of-the-year child profile which has information on the child's development in several important areas.

to complete, and they are able to read the entire book when it is finished. On each page is some tactile experience they have placed on the paper, along with a sentence that explains the work. "A is for apple" is written on the first page, with red apple prints smashed with paint from the apples we cut to see what was inside. They reread "B is for buttons" and remember the story of Corduroy, the bear who needed a button sewn on his overalls.

This book is placed in their portfolio at the end of the year, and helps them recall the activities we did and the books we read to make each letter meaningful and useful in their writing and reading.

The children also choose pieces of their other work we have collected, and conference with me periodically to explain the importance of each piece. This oral reflection on their work is somewhat of a celebration:

Not only do I see the growth in their work, but their ability to make choices and express their importance is always impressive.

More advanced students can take more responsibility in choosing what will go in their portfolios through written reflections about the work they select. This can be done in a number of ways, but the involvement of the students with their parents or guardians is another way of placing the responsibility for learning into the students' hands. When the students have completed an assessment of their own progress, they can then set new goals for their future learning development.

Terri Austin gives great detail about how she guides her students to conduct their own parent conferences in her book, *Changing the View.*

Much has been written about portfolio assessment, and this chapter is not intended as a lesson in how to use it with your students. The main point is to encourage its use, and to emphasize the role your students must take in compiling their portfolios if the portfolios are to be truly useful.

The list of books at the end of the chapter will help you locate resources to encourage productive portfolio assessment use.

Assessment Through Journals

I document my students' progress in their journals each month. I have adapted the "Lamme/Green Scale of Children's Development" (from Connie Green's research in compositional writing, 1987) to include the things I have noticed that are repetitive in my students' writing. (Fig. 5-4; reproducible on page 175). I have also added, in italics, notations showing development in drawing, for I have documented a progression in literacy development through my students' drawing, as well. For example, their sense of story and oral vocabulary show marked progress through more detailed drawings. As the year progresses, I am able to see how they repeat certain writing behaviors while making progress in others. Again, not only does this show me how far they have come, but it helps direct me to the most meaningful instruction for each child. I know just what to emphasize when working alone with one child, and can also see what mini-lessons I should give to the entire class. This type of evaluation exemplifies how my teaching and evaluation intertwine from day to day, each one directing the other.

Occasionally, I also make copies of journal entries as well as other written work. I write the child's name, the date, and a brief description of why I thought the writing sample was important to document. This al-

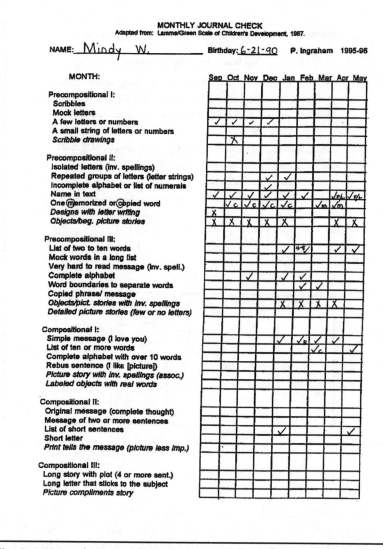

Fig. 5-4 Using this monthly journal check, a teacher can easily gauge a child's progress throughout the school year.

lows me to actually see each child's progress through the year. I include these in the child's portfolio along with any informal assessment given throughout the year. This portfolio provides me a more accurate picture of the development of each child. The information makes the job of evaluation and parent conferencing much easier, more accurate, and more informative.

Assessment in the Math Center

I also have a chart in my math center for tasks completed with manipulatives (Fig. 5-5; a modified version, on page 176, can be adapted for your use). When a child completes

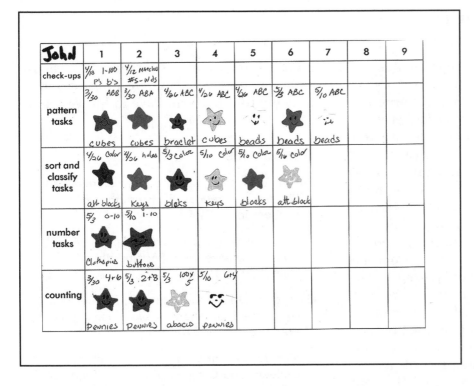

John	1	2	3	4	5	6	7	8	9
check-ups	4/10 1-100 P's b's	4/12 Matches #s-wds							
pattern tasks	3/30 ABB cubes	3/30 ABA cubes	4/26 ABC braclet	4/26 ABC cubes	4/26 ABC beads	5/3 ABC beads	5/10 ABC beads		
sort and classify tasks	4/26 Color alt blocks	4/26 holes Keys	5/3 color bloks	5/10 Color Keys	5/10 Color blocks	5/16 Color alt block			
number tasks	5/3 0-10 Clothspins	5/10 1-10 buttons							
counting	3/30 4+6 Pennies	5/3 2+8 Pennies	5/3 100x5 abacus	5/10 6+4 pennies					

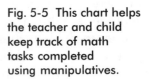

Fig. 5-5 This chart helps the teacher and child keep track of math tasks completed using manipulatives.

three to five tasks, depending on the time of year, she is to notify me. She gets her chart from the folder we keep at the math center, and I meet her there. While she explains each task and her process in completing it, I jot down the date, the materials she used, and some specific information about the task. These are actually anecdotal notations, but as they document specific work in the math center, I include them here.

As I check the child's work, I may ask her to do another task. If, for example, she is making only A-B patterns, and I feel she needs practice in more difficult ones, I would tell her to complete one A-B-C pattern for me before changing centers. Or, if she consistently uses the same materials for sorting and classification, I might ask her to complete a task using other materials.

By the end of the quarter, I have a chart describing the work each child has completed with the manipulatives in our math center. This documentation of the children's efforts is far more valuable to me than pulling them aside and drilling them in a one-shot assessment. I know that they can accomplish the specific skills in our curriculum, and I see that they are doing it in a challenging way on a regular basis.

Sometimes, of course, I see something different: When children are capable of completing work, but do not accomplish much, I have documentation to show their parents at our conference. These charts tell much more about each child than standardized testing, while alleviating the problem of setting aside extra time to assess the children's skills just to be able to fill out report cards.

Having a child explain his reasoning behind his work is a good way to assess his understanding of the skills and concepts involved.

Authentic Assessment of Progress

There is a place for standardized assessments when used as guideposts in a child's development. When things are not progressing for an individual, and the lack of progress is great enough to warrant outside intervention, it is critical that the child receives that help in a timely manner. Taking inventories or standardized assessments enables me to do this. My favorites are those devised by Marie Clay, and can be found in her book, *An Observation Survey of Early Literacy Achievement*. Giving such assessments as "Concepts About Print" or the "Test of Writing Vocabulary" at different times during the year allows me to examine each child's progress on an individualized and group-normed basis.

For children who are reading and writing with greater ability, running records are invaluable for documenting reading behaviors. Explanations of running records are given in a number of texts, and Rigby offers instructional videotapes along with its book, *Highlight My Strengths*, by Leanna Traill.

Excellent research in literacy assessment is documented in Lesley Mandel Morrow and Jeffrey Smith's book, *Assessment for Instruction in Early Literacy*. I have found this text invaluable in understanding the developmental stages of children's early literacy acquisition.

It is up to each teacher to choose the best means of assessing student achievement. It is helpful to make this decision with the assistance of teachers in other grade levels, if not as a total school, in order to be able to look at the child's growth over a period of years. While my own assessments are meaningful to me, it is advantageous to choose assessments that also give information to teachers the child will have in future years.

Resources

Austin, Terri. *Changing the View: Student-Led Parent Conferences.* Portsmouth, NH: Heinemann, 1994.

Clay, Marie M. *An Observation Survey of Early Literacy Achievement.* Portsmouth, NH: Heinemann, 1993.

Cochrane, Orin, and Cochrane, Donna. *Whole Language Evaluation for Classrooms.* Bothell, WA: The Wright Group, 1992.

Davies, Anne; Cameron, Caren; Politano, Colleen; and Gregory, Kathleen. *Together Is Better.* Winnipeg: Peguis, 1992.

Harp, Bill (Ed.) *Assessment and Evaluation in Whole Language Programs.* Norwood, MA: Christopher-Gordon Publishers, 1993.

"Lamme/Green Scale of Children's Development in Composition" from Green, C. (1987). *Assessing Kindergarten Children's Writing.* Unpublished research data.

Morrow, Lesley Mandel, and Smith, Jeffrey K. (Eds.) *Assessment for Instruction in Early Literacy.* Englewood Cliffs, NJ: Prentice Hall, 1990.

Tierney, Robert J.; Carter, Mark A.; and Desai, Laura E. *Portfolio Assessment in the Reading-Writing Classroom.* Norwood, MA: Christopher-Gordon Publishers, 1991.

Traill, Leanna. *Highlight My Strengths.* Crystal Lake, IL: Rigby, 1993.

Part 2

Learning Centers and Activities for Your Child-Centered Classroom

The next four chapters give explanations for setting up specific centers in your classroom, as well as suggested activities for each of those centers. No list is complete, but I have tried to give ideas for some tasks that could be used with a wide age and ability range. These will help get you started as you begin planning the activities for your thematic units.

The activities you choose to utilize should be meaningful and purposeful for your students in order to empower them to control their learning. The goal is not merely to keep your students busy. The goal is to find activities that are interesting, that link prior knowledge with new insight, and that allow room for creative achievement of the task. When the emphasis is placed on the process rather than the product, each child can be certain he or she will be able to meet with success. But be careful not to ignore the product. A job well done inspires us to work even harder. I think that's the key in empowering each child as an individual to push himself or herself to a new level.

In each activity, I have given the specific skills that the task will promote. Many activities encourage a multitude of skills, and depending on the time of year, I emphasize different ones. My intent in giving them is to demonstrate the way in which I include specific objectives in the activities I plan for center time. Depending on the way in which you use the ideas, your students' ages and needs, and the theme with which you use them, the specific objectives you have for each activity can easily change.

I will also show how one activity can be used for a variety of age and ability levels. As every class is filled with diverse individuals, the 🄜 symbol will be given to note ways to modify or adapt an activity for use with children having different chronological, developmental, or ability levels.

Terms such as "older" and "younger" children are not used, although they might apply. Younger children are often able to accomplish tasks older children may find difficult. I will leave it to each of you reading this book to decide how to use the activities with your students.

When introducing activities that have a variety of methods for completion, encourage each child to choose the most challenging work for her today. By emphasizing the word "today," you are letting all children know that what might be difficult today might be more easily accomplished tomorrow. It is not a matter of ability, but just a matter of time until each person will be able to accomplish even the most difficult task.

Literacy Development Centers

*Caleb read and read the letter so many times
that the ink began to run and the folds tore. He
read the book about sea birds over and over.*

— Patricia MacLachlan,
Sarah, Plain and Tall

I infuse reading and writing activities into every center, for we all use literacy skills to learn about math, science, and geography throughout our lives.

My students have reasons to read and write in the context of their block building, their dramatic play environments, and their games. These activities arise from the natural play experiences of my students, rather than as an alternative to other activities placed in that center. They are there to illustrate how we use literacy in our everyday lives, as well as to encourage further development of these skills.

However, I also incorporate specific literacy centers into my classroom, in order to give time and importance to the skills needed to become a literate adult.

- Our writing center provides creative writing opportunities, as well as encouraging legible handwriting.
- My library is used to promote reading for pleasure, and contains both fiction and nonfiction books.
- I often include space in my room for a journal center, even though we write in our journals as a whole class each day. I want children to be able to choose to add pages to their journal, or have more time to complete an entry.
- My language center relates our holistic language activities, books, poems, and songs with the specific skills children need to learn in order to become fluent readers and writers.

When making the decision as to which specific literacy centers to include in your classroom, think of your age group, your space, and the time you will allow for center time. Consider your specific goals in literacy, and design centers that will engage the children in meaningful activities that encourage those skills.

Specific objectives in vocabulary development, grammar, storytelling, spelling, and letter sounds can all be developed in language arts centers. Begin with the basics, and add other centers as you feel they are needed.

For example, journals can be kept in the writing center along with creative writing projects. Journaling should simply be a job each child accomplishes when he visits the writing center. He doesn't leave the center until he has completed both the creative writing task and his journal writing.

As the students begin to write regularly, they will spend more time at their journal entries. At the same time, they will choose more writing projects to develop and take through the editing process.

You will become better at conferencing, helping children move through writing tasks, conducting mini-lessons on specific skills, and suggesting more writing projects to individuals and the class as a group. When this happens, you might decide (as I did) that journals need to be given their own space and time. You then design an area for journaling, decide with the children what materials they will need in the center, and set it up.

Beyond the Emergent Stage of Writing

With students who are moving past the emergent stage, it is important to include writer's workshop and an extended reading period each day for every child. You might wish to set up a publishing center, rather than a writing center, where the students can publish their edited pieces of writing. Your library could be geared more toward a research center idea, explained more in Chapter 8, or change to highlight a specific genre or book the class is reading.

For example, if the thematic unit concerns our country's history, the class may be reading *Sarah, Plain and Tall*, by Patricia MacLachlan. The library center could contain additional books written about this period, as well as other books by MacLachlan herself. The children may wish to write letters to penpals, exchanging information about their area, just as Sarah did initially. Reports written by students, and art projects dealing with the unit, can be placed in the center for others to read. As your class changes themes, the reading center can be transformed to highlight each new book the class is sharing.

Word banks (Fig. 6-1) are listed in both the writing and journal centers, along with individual dictionaries. I receive many questions about word banking when I speak to teachers about writing activities with emergent writers.

I have found that I do not like to use word banks with young writers until they are hearing and using some consonant sounds to invent spellings. When I introduce word banks too early, my students begin to rely on me for spelling every word. They are more inclined to want it spelled "right."

I now wait to introduce word banking to those children who have begun using invented spelling to write new words. I allow them to ask one word at a time. This keeps them from asking, "How do you spell 'I went to the circus?'" too often. I help them realize which of those words they can spell on their own, then we see what words they might try to sound out. We usually wind up with one key word they want me to give them.

With emergents, I put the words on index cards, punch a hole in them, and place them on a ring. The first word I give them when I introduce them to this process is their own name, and this lets them identify their word bank. Each time I give them a new word, we add it to the ring, flip to their name, and they read every word in their bank to me. This helps build their sight vocabulary for reading and writing, and reminds them of the words they have asked for in the past that they might use again in their writing. We keep these in a small plastic basket in the journal center.

As the children move into the early stage of writing fluency, these rings become burdensome and impractical. I then suggest they use personal dictionaries they create, writing new words on an alphabetically ordered page.

These can be created by the teacher, or come commercially made. There are even some very nice ones for emergent writers that utilize pictures. I would recommend these especially in mixed-age classrooms that combine emergents with early and fluent writers, so that every child uses her own book for her words.

Whatever the method of keeping track of new words, the point is to help children have a fluent writing vocabulary and include more difficult words in their writing. I don't believe writing should be a struggle for young children. When I meet them along the way with words they can have at their fingertips, they are more inclined to write in sentences, sounding out words they need to complete their thoughts.

Using both invented spelling and word banks for writing allows children to reread their compositions with pride, knowing that they created many spellings but that key words are "correct." This spurs them on to memorize words that they use repeatedly and encourages a more rapid development of their personal writing vocabulary.

Whatever your situation, choose the literacy centers that work best to enhance your objectives and your students' day. Begin with one area that incorporates many activities, then add centers as specific needs arise. Ask your students to suggest new areas they wish were included in center time. Note which activities done in total group might be enhanced if included as a center, or might even be better accomplished as a center, rather than as a total class experience. Once your day is progressing, stop to assess what your students are accomplishing, and that will enable you to think of additional areas to add as a center.

Word Banks

Your child is bringing home her word bank today! This is a reminder of what this word bank is, and how you might put it to good use.

When your child is writing and needs a word spelled, I try one of two methods to help spell the word. One is known as invented spelling. This is tried on simple words that are fairly easy to sound out, such as "my." Very often, this is sounded out to spell "mi ," and that is fine. That is just how it sounds. Using invented spelling helps your child learn to become a speller, and this is something you want to encourage.

When the word your child wishes to write is more difficult, or is encountered after she has used invented spelling on several words, I spell the word for her. I do this to encourage the creative writing process and to help develop a sight vocabulary. Better readers and writers have a large sight vocabulary, and a child is most likely to remember words important to her. The words she chooses to use in her writing are words that have meaning for her, so this is a great way of choosing words to add to your child's sight vocabulary.

I write the word on an index card, punch a hole on the left side, and add it to the ring holding the cards. Whenever a new word is added to the word bank, we flip to the first word, and your child reads her word cards to me. I help sound out any that are unknown. This repeated reading of key words helps to build sight vocabulary for reading. Using this word bank during writing activities to find how to spell favorite words builds a writing vocabulary.

A key factor to the success of this project is that it is generated by your child. It should not be a mandatory activity each night before bed. It should not be used as a spelling list. Your child will learn to spell each word simply by using it over and over again.

So, now that you know the rules, congratulate your child on a job well done! She is blossoming into literacy, and that should be exciting and rewarding. Have a fun summer encouraging your child to write and appreciate her efforts by listening to her reread what she has written in her very own words!

Fig. 6-1 This letter to parents explains how using word banks helps children learn to spell.

THE WRITING CENTER

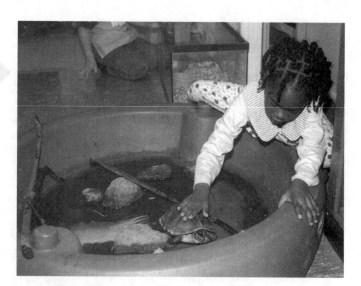

Keep a Topic List for Writing Ideas

◻ Have each child include a topic list of writing ideas in his portfolio, so he has something to write about on days when his mind cannot think of anything. Brainstorm and list these ideas as a group. Each child can keep these ideas with his writing portfolio, and can spend a few minutes adding new ideas to his list when he writes in this center, so that he is never in need of a topic to write on.

◻ Have the children write lists of what they are "experts" in. This will encourage the children to write on topics they know about. When the children share their lists of topics, it can give others ideas on things they know about, too.

Write About a Class Photograph

1. Take pictures of your students at work in your classroom on a regular basis.

2. Put the pictures out in the writing center.

3. Let each student choose a photograph to write about.

The pictures become the students' illustrations; they can write a narrative about what they do in school, and what they like about their classroom. These may be displayed to give other children ideas, or to show during a parent open house. They could also be combined or copied (if your students want to take their stories home or place them in their portfolios) to place in a class book. As the year goes by, this can become a class journal of your year together.

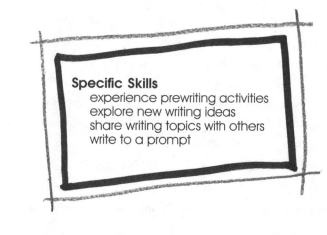

Specific Skills
experience prewriting activities
explore new writing ideas
share writing topics with others
write to a prompt

Create Alphabet Books for Thematic Units

◻ Students can create alphabet books independently, in small groups, or as a total class activity.

◻ Students can create their own books about a thematic topic by locating information for each letter of the alphabet. For each letter, have the student write two to five facts about the word. Illustrations may be drawn, cut from magazines, or photographs and postcards might be used.

◻ Older students can create an alphabet book as a culminating activity during a unit on the United States. Each student can choose a state to write about. For every letter of the alphabet, three facts should be included.

For example, in an alphabet book on Ohio, 'B' might look like this:

"B is for Buckeye."
The buckeye is the state tree.
People in Ohio sometimes carry a
"lucky buckeye" in their pocket.
The mascot at the Ohio State University
is a giant buckeye named Brutus Buckeye.

To encourage even more purposeful writing experiences, you can require students to use correspondence to investigate their state. They can write to the state government, the chamber of commerce, a local newspaper, or a specific tourist attraction.

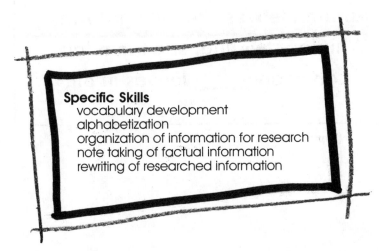

Specific Skills
vocabulary development
alphabetization
organization of information for research
note taking of factual information
rewriting of researched information

SUGGESTED MATERIALS

◻ small individual work table

◻ writing table for 4-6 people

◻ shelf for supplies

◻ dictionaries & picture dictionaries

◻ word banks, personal dictionaries, have-a-go sheets, or personal spelling lists

◻ chalkboard or dry-wipe board

◻ magnetic board, or side of a file cabinet

◻ small chalkboards or dry-wipe boards for trying out invented spellings

◻ word lists on charts

◻ student message board or mailboxes

◻ bulletin board to display completed projects and posters

◻ small file cabinet for writing portfolios

◻ teacher folders for conferencing and ongoing assessment

◻ chart stands for holding teacher-made & class-made charts, stories, and poems

◻ a variety of writing paper: unlined, lined, colored, letter writing paper, postcards, folded paper for greeting cards, sample handwriting models

◻ a variety of writing tools: pencils, erasers, markers, crayons, colored pencils, skinny markers, pens

◻ magnetic letters for invented spelling lessons/practice

◻ a computer and printer or word processor

◻ a variety of blank books

◻ personal cubbies for holding work, books, messages

◻ bulldog clips for hanging writing samples and models

◻ letter stamps and decorative stamps for designing special paper

◻ stapler, tape, paper fasteners

◻ letter trays or shoe cubbies for holding writing papers

Create Individual Interactive Charts

Interactive charts are large-print copies of short songs, poems, or verses taken from books to use regularly in the classroom. The charts become interactive through the use of manipulative word cards the child places in the verse. This enables the child to have some control over the activity.

Use of these charts offers children a risk-free environment to develop literacy skills at their own level of awareness. They provide successful participation in literacy activities. This fosters an enjoyment of the reading process, and negates fears some children have toward learning to read.

Using Interactive Charts

1. Introduce a book, song, or poem orally to the children. Allow children to feel comfortable with it through repetition.

2. Display the chart. Discover with the children that it is the printed form of what they have learned.

3. Recite the contents of the chart together, pointing to each word.

4. Allow the children to volunteer leading the group in reading the chart, using the pointer as they read.

5. Place the chart where the children can easily use it.

6. Allow the children opportunities to recreate the chart to take home.

Examples of Books Good for Creating Interactive Charts:

Creature Features
Brown Bear, Brown Bear, What Do You See?
Sitting in My Box
It Looked Like Spilt Milk
Dear Zoo
The Very Hungry Caterpillar
It Didn't Frighten Me!
Chicka Chicka Boom Boom

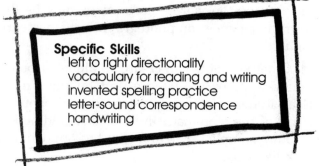

Specific Skills
left to right directionality
vocabulary for reading and writing
invented spelling practice
letter-sound correspondence
handwriting

Autumn Leaves

Red and yellow, orange and brown,
Autumn leaves are falling down.
Whirling, twirling, see them fall.
I can count_____leaves in all!

(Reproducible on page 177)

Recreate Individual *Goodnight Moon* Books

(or another favorite book)

1. Read the book *Goodnight Moon*, by Margaret Wise Brown, several times.
2. Discuss with the children what their bedtime routines are.
3. List with the children all the people and things in their bedrooms that they say goodnight to, in order to prolong bedtime.
4. Create blank *Goodnight Moon* papers and place them in the writing center.

5. Demonstrate to the class how to complete the pages, using invented spelling to write in the word they will say goodnight to, and illustrating the word(s).
6. Encourage the children to complete several pages over the next week or two. Keep the completed papers together un-til each child has completed all the pages she is able to.
7. Have the children design covers (front and back) out of gray construction paper. (This might be completed in the art center.) Some children might need help compiling the pages of the book. Staple pages together.
8. Ask each child to reread her own book to you and other children in the class. Invite older children into the room to listen to the children reread their books.
9. Have an authors' sharing time, and encourage each child to read his book to the class.

Specific Skills
recreate fiction and nonfiction books
develop invented spelling strategies
develop sight vocabulary in reading and writing

Use Writing to Correspond With Others

◎ Write pen pals in other states or another classroom across town.

◎ Create cards for every occasion. Keep a stack of blank cards that the children may use for friends and family members.

◎ Before each child's birthday, the class could make birthday cards.

◎ Have each child make an invitation for PTA meetings, Open House, plays and musical performances, Author's Teas, etc.

◎ Invite students to periodically write stories about the activities in their classroom to send to the local newspaper. Include a photograph.

◎ Write thank-you cards to visitors, speakers, parents who chaperone field trips, grandparents who come to read, adults who volunteer, custodians and school secretaries who help the students in special ways.

Specific Skills
use writing as correspondence
compose writing for a purpose

Create an Ending for *Do Not Open*
(or another trade book*)

1. Read the book *Do Not Open*, by Brinton Turkle, stopping just as Miss Moody is wondering whether or not to open the bottle. (* Any book may be substituted in this activity.)

2. Ask the children to decide what is in the bottle, and what happens to Miss Moody and Captain Kidd when she opens it. Have each child complete his own ending to the story at the writing center, complete with illustrations. Length should depend upon age level of students, as this story appeals to a wide enough range to use with kindergartners through sixth graders.

3. Display endings.

4. Read the rest of the book so the children know how Brinton Turkle chose to complete the story. Discuss his use of mood, choosing to make the story both scary and humorous. Discuss the message of courage and Miss Moody's choice to trick the monster.

Specific Skills
write for a variety of reasons
use invented spelling strategies
develop vocabulary
apply knowledge of beginning,
    middle, and end
write to a given prompt
experience writing in a variety of genres

Create Picture Dictionaries or Spelling Dictionaries

These can be created as a group project, or they can be personal dictionaries for the children to use while writing. Several companies publish these to use in the classroom, or teachers may choose to create them with the students by making blank books. The students can write the alphabet (one letter per page) at the top of the page. These could be used in conjunction with your spelling program, as each child finds words to learn to spell correctly in her own writing.

Specific Skills
letter recognition
sound-symbol awareness
alphabetical order
development of writing,
vocabulary, and spelling skills

Create Thematic Vocabulary Books

Create small books (or Big Books) using vocabulary words the students are learning independently or as a class. These may be words related to a thematic unit, homonyms, rhyming words, words from their word banks, or whatever area you choose to use in order to nurture strong vocabularies in reading and writing.

Modify this task for different levels by requiring the children to choose vocabulary words from their writing or reading. They may simply place the word alone on the page, draw a picture to define the word, or write a definition. They could also use each word in a sentence within the context of your unit.

Specific Skills
vocabulary development
writing nonfiction
writing complete sentences

Create an Informational Step Book Related to Your Thematic Unit

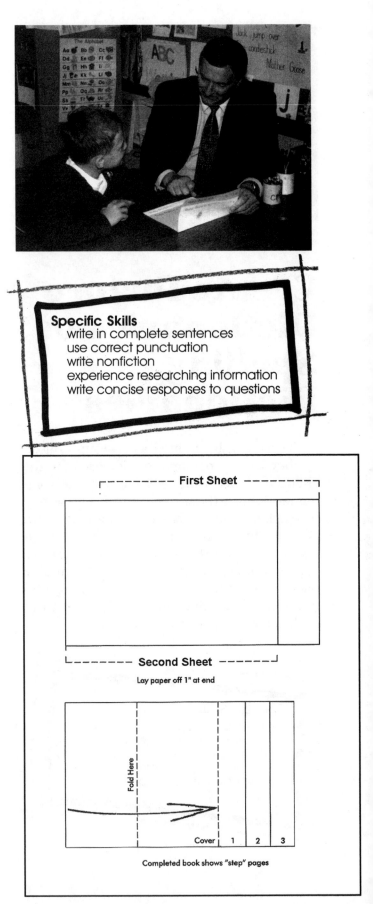

Fold paper to create step books as shown in the illustration. On each step write a question you have had about your unit. Open the page to answer each question in a sentence, using illustrations when possible.

 Modify this task for different levels by providing questions on charts or printed on the step books. Some children might choose to simply answer the questions inside each page, using a four-page step book.

Students needing a more challenging task can create their own questions, possibly using a six- or eight-page step book.

Specific Skills
write in complete sentences
use correct punctuation
write nonfiction
experience researching information
write concise responses to questions

┌────── **First Sheet** ──────┐

─────── **Second Sheet** ───────
Lay paper off 1" at end

Fold Here

Cover | 1 | 2 | 3

Completed book shows "step" pages

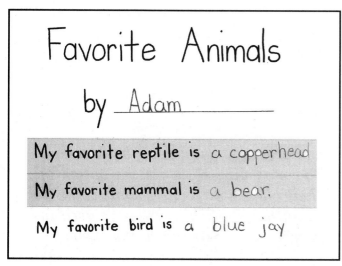

Favorite Animals

by Adam

My favorite reptile is a copperhead

My favorite mammal is a bear.

My favorite bird is a blue jay

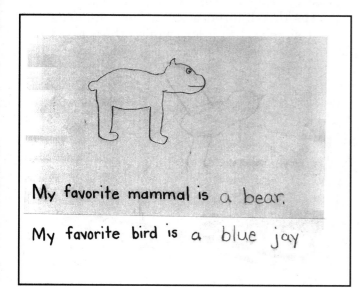

My favorite mammal is a bear.

My favorite bird is a blue jay

Use Writing Portfolios

Particularly in the elementary grades, children should begin to learn how to keep a writing portfolio and choose projects to edit, revise, and publish. There are numerous books to help teachers begin this process with their students. Some I highly recommend include:

> *A Fresh Look at Writing*, by Donald Graves (K -12)
> *Joyful Learning*, by Bobbi Fisher (K - 1)
> *Invitations*, by Regie Routman (K - 6)
> *In the Middle*, by Nancie Atwell (5 - 9)

In classrooms where writer's workshop is a part of each day, portfolios could be kept in a writing, publishing, or conferencing center. This area could be used to give extended opportunities for children to write. Or, the writing center could highlight different genres as the year progresses. In this way, children can write freely during writer's workshop, but have more guidelines at the writing center.

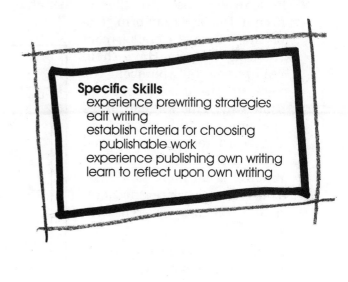

Specific Skills
experience prewriting strategies
edit writing
establish criteria for choosing
    publishable work
experience publishing own writing
learn to reflect upon own writing

THE LIBRARY/READING CENTER

Each activity listed can be tied to your thematic unit by placing books about that theme in your library/reading center. You may give students the option of completing these activities with any book of their choice, or require some tasks to be completed with books from the theme shelf. Author studies can also be used in this way, encouraging reading books by a specific author linked to the theme in some way.

Reading Logs

◉ Create reading logs for students to keep track of their reading. Have the students use these to reflect upon their reading development.

◉ Make copies of reading logs for each child.

◉ Decorate a file folder with pictures of books appropriate to your students' reading levels. Laminate the folder or cover it in clear adhesive paper.

◉ Demonstrate how the children should keep track of the reading they do each time they visit the library.

◉ Periodically, check the file and ask children in the library to bring one of their favorite books from their list to you. Have them read to you, tell you about the book, or discuss the book in some way. This will encourage the children to participate in the record-keeping process, and show them that independent reading is an important task. You can also write anecdotal notes on their progress as they read.

◉ Place the folder in the library with pencil and eraser.

Ⓜ Modify this task for a variety of ability levels by varying the types of reading responses the children create. Some students might simply keep a log, while others could write a sentence or a paragraph about their reading.

Specific Skills
spend time reading
choose appropriate material for
   reading
reflect upon reading improvement

Reading Log

Name _Lauren_

Date	Title of the book	Tell me about the book	☺ ☹
	M very First Book	WRsa	☺
	Pet animals	animals	☺
	Eeeee k!		☺
	Brown Bear	Cairs.	☺
	ACROSS THE STREAM	God	☺

(Reproducible on page 178)

Read with Study Buddies

- Arrange with another teacher to trade students periodically. As a center activity, children can be assigned days and times to visit their buddy's classroom to encourage oral reading skills. This can be done with a mixture of age groups.

- Include activities like: oral reading, storytelling, reader's theater, poetry sharing, dramatic retellings of stories.

Specific Skills
listening to others read
reacting orally to a book
improving reading strategies
developing vocabulary

- regular bookshelf with a wide range of books, spanning several levels of reading ability, and including wordless picture books at every level for language development

- display bookshelf with books recently read to the class, books published by the class, small versions of big books, and books that are of current interest to the class

- comfortable seating, such as a rocking chair (adult-sized for volunteers to read to children, and child-sized), bean bag chair, pillows, carpet, or carpet squares

- stuffed animals to read to — these might include some of the many storybook characters out today, such as the bunny in Goodnight Moon, Paddington Bear, Corduroy, Madeline, Max and the Wild Things, Pooh Bear, Clifford, etc.

- listening center: books and music on tapes with tape recorder and headphones for one to three people. (Tapes do not have to be commercially made. Read the story with your class, having them help during predictable passages or cumulative segments, and tape as you read. Place the tape in the listening corner.)

- interactive charts

- literature logs, reading response journals, and/or forms for keeping track of the books each child reads

- small table or desk for writing in literature logs, etc.

- pencils and erasers for writing in literature logs, reading response journals, and reading forms

- posters and poetry charts as reading incentives

- Big Book pocket holders (the ones that hang on the wall and are simply big pockets take up little room and hold the books nicely)

- small (child-sized) chart stands for Big Books and interactive charts

- flannel board with sets to retell favorite stories

- puppets (possibly to go with a book)

- check-out cards and date stamp to allow the children to borrow books to read at home (older children can run this independently)

- canvas or plastic library bags for carrying borrowed books

Compare & Contrast Two Books

Here I teach a lesson on Venn diagrams to the whole class. I then place blank Venn diagrams in the learning centers for use with various activities.

◙ Place Venn diagrams in the reading/library center, marked at the top with "characters," "plot," and "setting."

◙ Ask the children to compare and contrast two books, using one of the criteria. This might be a generic job, for a period of time, that each child must do whenever visiting the reading or library center. Reading critically, with character, plot, and setting as a focus, will then become an easier task.

Specific Skills
compare and contrast
    characters, plot, or setting
read critically
use graphic organizers to
    respond to reading

Name *Brad*

I am comparing the: (**characters**) **plot** **setting** of these books

Dear Rebecca, Winter is Here   *Dear Mr. Henshaw*

a grown up is the main character

She is telling how the seasons chang

Throughout the book she writes a letter

Started as letters

Both were writing to someone they cared about

a kid is the main character.

He asked questions about how to write stories

In the middle of the book he starts a journal

Read a Variety of Genres

- Have the students keep a log on the types of books they are reading, according to the genre.

- Discuss with the people at the center which genres they enjoy most, explaining why and giving suggestions for books in this genre.

- Have students read a book recommended by a friend in a genre they have not previously tried.

- Try dividing the class into cooperative groups according to the children's favorite types of books. Ask each child to report to her group about her favorite book within that genre so that she can share a book of common interest to her group members. The group as a whole can then report to the class what common characteristics it enjoys about its books, and why others in the class might also like to try reading one of these books.

Specific Skills
read a variety of genres
respond orally to reading
compare and contrast books

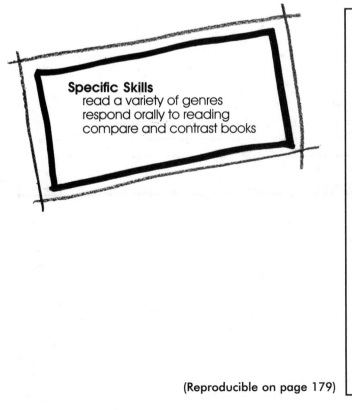

Class Reading Log
Genre: Poetry

Date	Reader	Title of Book	Comments
10-6	Katie	Hey World, Here I am!	Very good
10-12	La'tisha	Brown Angles	good use of words
10-28	Adam	Where the Sidewalk ends	hilarious
11-13	Brad	How Old is Old?	very funny
12-1	Kevin	How Beastly	I liked the pictures

Class Reading Log
Genre: Science Fiction

Date	Reader	Title of Book	Comments
9-11	Joey	The Green Book	This book was very good.
10-1	Amber	Star Wars	Michael liked this book very well.
10-16	Mr. T.	The Truce at Bakura	The author used very descriptive words
11-3	Matt	Aliens ate My Homework	I loved the end
12-10	Adam	Return of the Jedi	This is the best one in the series
1-11	Rachel	Stinker from Space	a great book

(Reproducible on page 179)

Complete Beginning-Middle-End Retelling

When reading in the center, children complete a sheet retelling the beginning, middle, and end of a story they have read.

m Modify this task for different levels by allowing multiple forms of responding, including illustrations for emergents to detailed paragraphs for fluent readers. Provide different forms to allow choice.

Specific Skills
comprehension
retelling events in a story
sequencing events
applying knowledge of beginning-
  middle-end

Tell Me the Story

Charlie Anderson

First,	Next,	Last,

Name ___

☺ I liked this story.   ☹ I did not like this story.

(Reproducible pages for both worksheets can be found on pages 180 and 181.)

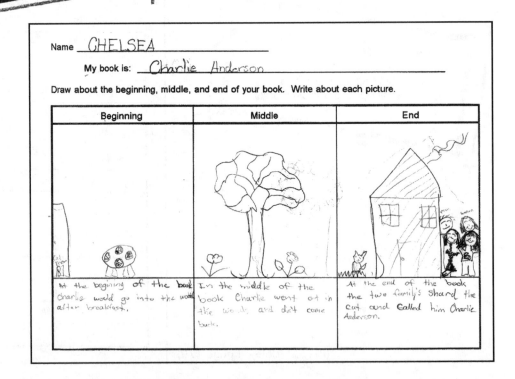

Name CHELSEA

My book is: Charlie Anderson

Draw about the beginning, middle, and end of your book. Write about each picture.

Beginning	Middle	End
At the beginning of the book charlie would go into the woods after breakfast.	In the middle of the book Charlie went ot in the woods and didt come back.	At the end of the book the two family's shard the cat and called him charlie Anderson.

Reading Response Logs

These may be encouraged during SSR/DEAR time, and/or kept in the library center to complete at that time, if you prefer to use some other reporting measures for the children's regular reading program.

- Demonstrate for the children how to write a brief paragraph or two about each passage they read when they visit the library.

- Discuss what might be written, possibly using examples on an overhead. This process should be done consistently as the children progress in their reading, writing, and comprehension ability.

- Have each child bring in his own three-ring binder, or use spiral notebooks. Set aside space in the library center for these.

- At least once a week, write a response or suggestion to each child about his reading topic or his writing about his reading. These might best be done progressively, assigning four or five students to read and write, and immediately respond to each day's writing.

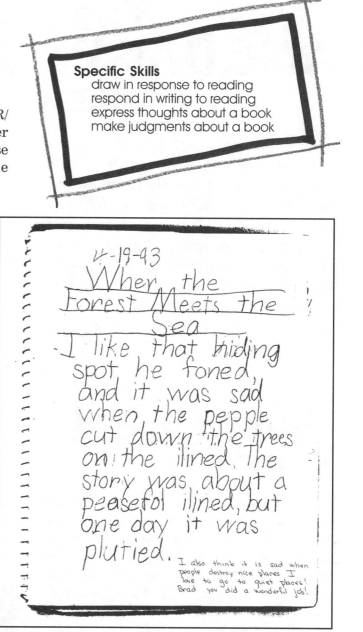

> 4-19-93
> Wher the Forest Meets the Sea
> - I like that hiding spot he foned, and it was sad when the pepple cut down the trees on the ilined. The story was about a peasefol ilined, but one day it was plutied.
>
> I also think it is sad when people destroy nice places I love to go to quiet places! Brad you did a wonderful job!

Books on Tape

Put books on tapes into center with small headphones so children can listen while they read along.

THE LANGUAGE CENTER

This center will allow you to include activities and games that enable the children to practice specific literacy skills. Children can play word and language games that you have placed into the center after completing a specific task that is appropriate for your students.

Flannel Board Words

Place words written on sentence strips onto a flannel board. Children can rewrite each word with flannel board letters. These words might be used in thematic journals, rewritten on a chalkboard or dry-wipe board, or on a sheet of paper when all are completed. This creates a permanent record of each word list for every child.

Specific Skills
vocabulary development
spelling
handwriting

Create a Word Game

▣ Create a list of vocabulary words from the children's thematic unit or literature book that they would like to learn to spell.
▣ Instruct each child to make a game to help him learn these words. Show several word games as models, such as "Go Fish" or "Concentration."

Ⓜ Modify this task for different levels by matching words to definitions, rather than simply matching words.

Specific Skills
vocabulary development
higher-level thinking strategies
oral language development
cooperative group strategies

Little Letter Books

Complete books about words that begin with a certain letter when highlighting that letter/sound.

Specific Skills
letter recognition
sound-symbol awareness
vocabulary development
conventions of print

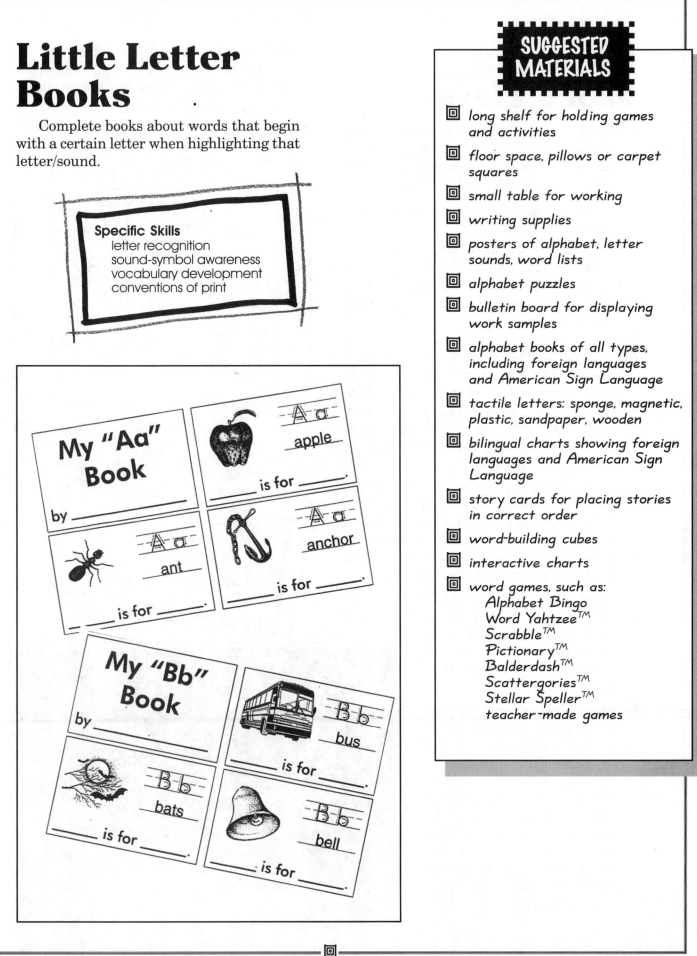

SUGGESTED MATERIALS

- long shelf for holding games and activities
- floor space, pillows or carpet squares
- small table for working
- writing supplies
- posters of alphabet, letter sounds, word lists
- alphabet puzzles
- bulletin board for displaying work samples
- alphabet books of all types, including foreign languages and American Sign Language
- tactile letters: sponge, magnetic, plastic, sandpaper, wooden
- bilingual charts showing foreign languages and American Sign Language
- story cards for placing stories in correct order
- word-building cubes
- interactive charts
- word games, such as:
    Alphabet Bingo
    Word Yahtzee™
    Scrabble™
    Pictionary™
    Balderdash™
    Scattergories™
    Stellar Speller™
    teacher-made games

My "Aa" Book
by _____

A a
apple
_____ is for _____.

A a
ant
_____ is for _____.

A a
anchor
_____ is for _____.

My "Bb" Book
by _____

B b
bus
_____ is for _____.

B b
bats
_____ is for _____.

B b
bell
_____ is for _____.

Rhyming Word Lists

◉ Make a poster-sized version of the chart. Choose a word you would like your class to rhyme. According to your goals for this lesson, you might choose words:

- that demonstrate a short vowel sound, such as bat, hat, fat
- that will allow studying a long vowel word family, such as like, bike, hike
- that will lead to rhymes for use in a thematic poem, such as ocean, lotion, emotion

◉ Ask the children to give you words that rhyme with the word in the box. Write the words down in the first column so that the children see the correct spelling (some words that rhyme are not spelled with the same pattern of letters, for example, "moon" and "June").

◉ After writing the word in the first column, have the child who suggests the word re-write it in the middle column and then draw a picture of it in the third column. These lists may be placed in the writing center for poetry or journal writing.

◉ This lesson might also begin with the child writing a rhyming word using invented spelling strategies; the teacher can then rewrite the word using "adult" or conventional spelling.

◉ Blank forms may also be placed in the language center so that children may use them to create their own lists of rhyming words to use in their writing folder. Instruct the children to try spelling the word on their own in the middle column, then have the list checked by another student or the teacher. The correct spelling may then be written in the

first column. Later, the children can use this list in their writing folders, seeing the difference between their invented spellings and the correct spellings.

(Reproducible on page 182)

Specific Skills
vocabulary development
spelling patterns
rhyming words
invented spelling strategies
phonetic rules

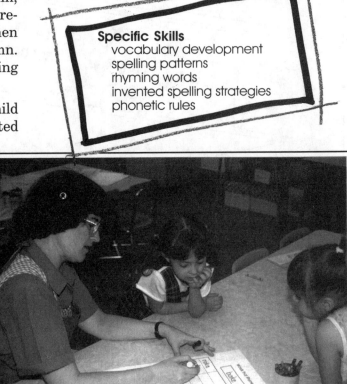

Spell the Word or Name Games

◙ Place envelopes in the language center containing letters that spell words important to the class. For kindergartners, these might simply be the names of the children in your class; for children in the primary grades, they could be words they are learning in a thematic unit.

◙ On the outside of the envelope, write the word the child should spell and place a picture of the word. (School photographs work well for name envelopes; stickers of objects work well for thematic words, such as transportation vehicles, animals, continents or countries.)

◙ Make individual letters which spell the words, and place them in the envelopes. You may make the letters by cutting 3 x 5 index cards into fourths, so that they are similar to tiny flashcards.

The envelopes and letters can be used in a number of ways:

• Students can look at the word on the front of the envelope and recreate the word with the letters inside.

• More advanced students can turn the envelope face down and test their ability to spell the word with the letters inside the envelope.

• Children can take the letters out of the envelope one by one without looking at the front of the envelope, and figure out what word is spelled with those letters.

Specific Skills
vocabulary development
letter recognition
letter-sound correspondence
invented spelling strategies
phonetic rules

THE JOURNAL CENTER

Writing Response Journals

◙ Utilize the journal center for writing response journals with your children. When this is done as a center activity, the number of children needing to have you write responses is limited each day. This helps the teacher keep up with responses to each child's journal.

◙ Periodically exchange names to involve the students in response journals with one another.

Specific Skills
express feelings or ideas in written
    form
explain one's position in writing to
    another person
respond in writing to another person

Write About a Drawing

Encourage the children to draw a detailed picture about an event in their lives or a favorite book, then use "letter writing" to tell about the picture in words. Using the term "letter writing" will enable emergent writers to feel positive about their writing, even though they might only be putting down favorite letters. At the same time, this will encourage beginning writers to attempt writing to an audience, as in writing a letter to a friend.

Specific Skills
compose stories through
    drawing and writing
develop writing vocabulary
tell or retell favorite stories in detail
develop compositional writing skills
write in complete sentences

Creating Prompts

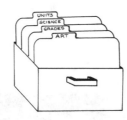

Invite the students to write new writing ideas on blank index cards to be placed in the prompt box. These might be questions about a book, a poem, a proverb, a personal question — the possibilities are endless.

(Modeling this might encourage your students to choose to take part in this activity.)

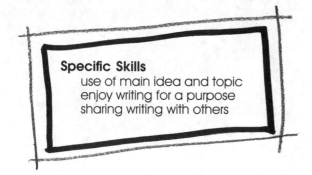

Specific Skills
use of main idea and topic
enjoy writing for a purpose
sharing writing with others

Message Boards

Require children to write one short message to a friend while at the journal center. This might consist of a pat on the back for something she did well, or to ask a question. Notes may be pinned to a board, left in file folders, or placed in orange juice container cubbies.

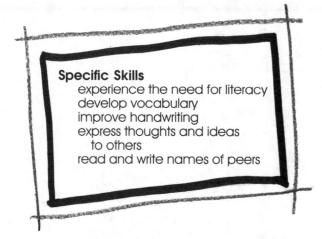

Specific Skills
experience the need for literacy
develop vocabulary
improve handwriting
express thoughts and ideas
   to others
read and write names of peers

Personal Journals

Have the children keep personal journals, reflecting on their own thoughts and activities. Prompts may be given for children to use as an option. Encouraging the use of drawing to organize thoughts and reflections can help reluctant writers know where to begin.

Examples of open-ended questions for prompts:

- ▣ Who would make an excellent President of the USA?

- ▣ Who is your best friend? Name the five qualities that he or she has that make you like him or her.

- ▣ How can we improve lunch period; how can we improve our cafeteria?

- ▣ What is the best job in the world? Why?

- ▣ What would you change about our classroom if you could?

- ▣ If you were our teacher, what would our daily schedule be?

- ▣ Make a list of three places you would like to visit, and explain why.

- ▣ What can you do this week to improve the world?

- ▣ What did you do last week that improved the world?

- ▣ What is the greatest invention known to man? Why?

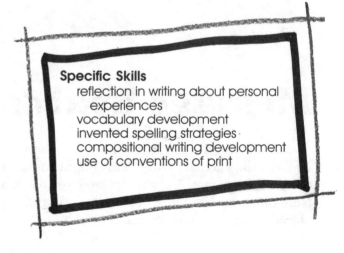

Specific Skills
reflection in writing about personal experiences
vocabulary development
invented spelling strategies
compositional writing development
use of conventions of print

Thematic Journals

- Have children write in thematic journals, encouraging them to reflect upon their learning in the content areas through a written response.

- Have children share responses with others in the center and explain vocabulary words each has chosen. Express thoughts and questions about the theme orally.

- Use the form shown here to help students report on their thematic learning.

Thematic Unit: The Solar System

Name: Chelsea   Date: Jan. 10 '96

New vocabulary words I can use:

1. Craters   2. Oxygen   3. Sulfur

I discovered that Venus is hoter than Mercury because Venus has Sulfur clouds. They keo the heat in.

My favorite activity was Team teaching Day

(Reproducible on page 183)

Specific Skills
vocabulary development
personal reflection about learning
discussion of information
   with others
expression of thoughts and
   views on new information

◙ Chapter 6 ◙

Teacher Resources

Adams, Marilyn Jager. *Beginning to Read: Thinking and Learning about Print*. Cambridge, MA: The MIT Press, 1990.

Atwell, Nancie. *In the Middle: Writing, Reading, and Learning with Adolescents*. Portsmouth, NH: Heinemann, 1987.

Clay, Marie M. *Becoming Literate: The Construction of Inner Control*. Portsmouth, NH: Heinemann, 1991.

——. *What Did I Write?* Portsmouth, NH: Heinemann,1975.

Fisher, Bobbi. *Joyful Learning: A Whole Language Kindergarten*. Portsmouth, NH: Heinemann, 1991.

Fletcher, Ralph. *What a Writer Needs*. Portsmouth, NH: Heinemann, 1993.

——. *A Writer's Notebook: Unlocking the Writer Within You*. New York: Avon Books, 1996.

Gentry, J. Richard, and Gillet, Jean Wallace. *Teaching Kids to Spell*. Portsmouth, NH: Heinemann, 1993.

Graves, Donald H. *A Fresh Look at Writing*. Portsmouth, NH: Heinemann, 1994.

——. *Build a Literate Classroom*. Portsmouth, NH: Heinemann, 1991.

Heard, Georgia. *For the Good of the Earth and Sun*. Portsmouth, NH: Heinemann, 1989.

McGee, Lea M., and Richgels, Donald J. *Literacy's Beginnings: Supporting Young Readers and Writers*.Boston: Allyn and Bacon, 1990.

Morrow, Lesley Mandel. *Literacy Development in the Early Years*. Englewood Cliffs, NJ: Prentice Hall, 1989.

Routman, Regie. *Invitations: Changing as Teachers and Learners*. Portsmouth, NH: Heinemann, 1991, 1994.

——. *Transitions: From Literature to Literacy*. Portsmouth, NH: Heinemann, 1988.

Schlosser, Kristen G., and Phillips, Vicki L. *Beginning in Whole Language: A Practical Guide*. New York: Scholastic, 1991.

——. *Building Literacy with Interactive Charts*. New York: Scholastic.

Strickland, Dorothy S., and Morrow, Lesley Mandel (Eds.) *Emerging Literacy: Young Children Learn to Read and Write*. Newark, DE: International Reading Association, 1989.

Children's Trade Books

Abercrombie, Barbara. *Charlie Anderson*. New York: Aladdin Paperbacks, 1995.

Brown, Margaret Wise. *Goodnight Moon*. New York: Harper & Row, 1947.

Campbell, Rod. *Dear Zoo*. New York: Puffin Books, 1982.

Carle, Eric. *The Very Hungry Caterpillar*. New York: Philomel: 1969.

Goss, Janet L., and Harste, Jerome C. *It Didn't Frighten Me!* Worthington, OH: Willowisp Press, 1985.

Lillegard, Dee. *Sitting in My Box*. New York: Puffin Books, 1989.

MacLachlan, Patricia. *Sarah, Plain and Tall*. New York: Harper & Row, 1985.

Martin, Bill, Jr. *Brown Bear, Brown Bear, What Do You See?* New York: Henry Holt, 1983.

Martin Bill, Jr., and Archambault, John. *Chicka Chicka Boom Boom*. New York: Simon & Schuster, 1989.

Shaw, Charles G. *It Looked Like Spilt Milk*. New York: Scholastic, 1988.

Turkle, Brinton. *Do Not Open*. New York: E.P. Dutton, 1981.

Additional Resources for Center Ideas and Activities

Idea Books:

Brumbaugh, Brenda, and Thompson-Trenta, Nan. *Listening for Basic Concepts All Year 'Round*. East Moline, IL: LinguiSystems, 1990.

Johnson, Paul. *A Book of One's Own: Developing Literacy Through Making Books*. Portsmouth, NH: Heinemann, 1990.

McElmeel, Sharron L. *The Poet Tree*. Englewood, CO: Teacher Ideas Press, 1993.

Moen, Christine Boardman. *Better Than Book Reports* (Grades 2-6). New York: Scholastic, 1992.

Nyberg, Judy. *Charts for Children: Print Awareness Activities for Young Children*. Glenview, IL: GoodYear Books, 1996.

Poppe, Carol A., and VanMatre, Nancy A. *Language Arts Learning Centers for the Primary Grades*. West Nyack, NY: Center for Applied Research in Education, 1991.

Wait, Shirleen S. *Reading Learning Centers For the Primary Grades*. West Nyack, NY: Center for Applied Research in Education, 1992.

Sources for Blank Journals and Personal Word Dictionaries

Curriculum Associates, Inc.
5 Esquire Road
N. Billerica, MA 01862-2589
1-800-225-0248

Zaner-Bloser, Inc.
P.O. Box 16764
Columbus, OH 43216-6764
1-800-421-3018

Creative Journals

Ingraham, Phoebe Bell. *My ABC Journal: An Emergent Literacy Journal*. Columbus, OH: Zaner-Bloser, 1996. Individual journals for emergents that offer writing ideas for each letter of the alphabet.

Write Away! Journals
Blooming Publications
P.O. Box 2178
Bloomington, IN 47402
1-800-489-9933

Games

Alphabet Bingo can be found at most teacher stores or in most teacher catalogs.

Stellar Speller™ is a Discovery Toy.

Scrabble™, *Balderdash*™ , *Word Yahtzee*™, *Pictionary*™, and *Scattergories*™ can be found at any toy store or in most department store toy departments.

Cognitive Development Centers

Once there was a bird named Bry. She liked to fly. She liked to fly home to her tree.

—words to a tangram tale
by Jessica Lackey, age 6

I include math, science, and geography in my cognitive development centers. These subjects have specific objectives which I teach throughout the year, and so they each have space in my classroom.

While each area has some generic manipulatives that stay out in the center all year, other materials come and go with each thematic unit. Literacy activities (books, poems, interactive charts, and writing tasks) are also found in each of these centers throughout the year. These tasks are usually designed around the thematic unit, integrating the curriculum around a central topic.

My thematic units are primarily based on science concepts, so this portion of the room brings together many of the activities found throughout the classroom. I have found that science concepts are usually broad enough to allow me to integrate my curriculum more easily than with any other content area, without having to stretch too far to find activities relevant to the topic.

In the past, my units lasted about a month. I have now moved to quarterly themes, with mini-units within these themes that tie together and flow nicely from one to the next. This allows me to change materials in my centers gradually, leaving some favorite tasks from the previous unit out as we begin to study the next concept.

I can keep the same units intact from year to year, but focus attention on different aspects at any time. For example, during a unit on living things, we might discover that many children have visited the beach recently. From their interest, we can begin a study of life in the ocean. The science center would then hold tasks and manipulatives to help the children discover what life is like in the ocean. A science experiment investigating the concepts of "sink" and "float" could be used here.

In the geography center, we could study the oceans of the world and possibly the continent of Australia, in order to learn more about the Great Barrier Reef.

Math activities could include conservation activities, pouring and measuring liquids, classification tasks using seashells and other sea creatures, counting and creating patterns with shells, and predicting activities of size and weight with shells.

Literacy is included in each of these areas as we make graphs, read and write about our learning, create interactive charts and books about sea creatures, and master specific language skills by using them in our literacy activities. In this way, all centers are tied together with a common thread of interest and thought, while the specific goals you have in each subject area are also addressed.

Pouring and measuring activities are suitable for both math and science centers.

Opening Expectations

I don't necessarily leave out units or concepts if my students fail to show an interest in them. Some children are too shy to make suggestions or let me know what's going on inside their heads, or have just never been introduced to that particular topic. While some educators feel that you can't teach a young child something that he has no prior experience or knowledge of, I disagree.

Certainly, a young child won't be able to appreciate the vastness of the ocean unless she experiences it herself. But if I never teach my children about the ocean simply because we live in Ohio and don't have regular "ocean experiences," my students might never be enticed to visit it. If I don't teach them that there are faraway places where people live who have many interesting beliefs and customs, how will they ever learn to appreciate those places?

Certainly, units that hold completely new information for my students have a different focus: They become introductory experiences that lay a foundation for the future, rather than being very specific and filled with information for the child to master. The way in which I introduce the child to new information will be adjusted, using concrete experiences and manipulatives.

It is easy for teachers, in the attempt to protect students from failure and embarrassment, to underestimate their ability to learn something new. I try to avoid this — not that I want them to fail or to be embarrassed. Instead, I create a classroom environment where we respect and trust each other. I model attitudes that tell my children it is all right to fail, and that failure is often our best teacher. I want my students to take risks in their learning, and to become open to new experiences, different ideas, and people who are not just like them in every way.

One way I do this is through trying new things with the class. A few years ago, I decided to have my students learn the American Sign Language alphabet. It is a very kinesthetic tool for learning about letters, as well as an interesting way for students to experience how we can overcome difficulties and disabilities. I had no experience with sign language, but we jumped in together. Often, the children did much better than I did, and they let me know it. But I kept trying.

One day, a group of teachers from a Cincinnati school visited our classroom. One of the teachers happened to be deaf, and she and her interpreter were gracious enough to teach us to sing the Alphabet Song from beginning to end, using sign language. The children practiced it throughout the year, and were very proud of their effort. Not only did I find that it helped many of my students learn letter recognition, but it brought about a feeling of closeness in our group as we undertook this difficult task together. It also became a common thread that carried a feeling of respect for others throughout the year.

Whatever centers you choose to place in your classroom, I advise you to find a common thread among them that will offer group experiences to help you and your students form a cohesive unit. It might be learning about world geography or learning a foreign language, possibly from a foreign exchange student. It will enhance your students' learning and experience, and may even solve all sorts of discipline and motivational difficulties you've been frustrated with in past years.

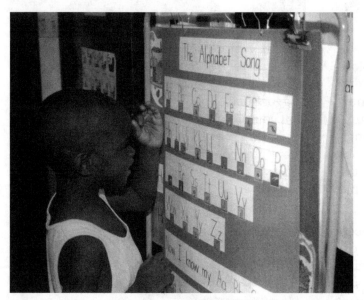

A kindergarten student practices American Sign Language.

THE MATH CENTER

Free Exploration of Math Manipulatives

To begin the year, this center may be opened from the first day, as children explore what can be done with the materials. I like to discuss what a mathematician does, and how he or she solves problems with space, numbers, and shapes. I tie this in with my modeling in the block center, for I like to point out the thinking process that needs to take place as the children build, if they want to build something specific.

Demonstrating the behaviors I'm expecting in each center allows the children to explore work on their own without my telling them exactly what to do, but setting limits so that the activity is directed toward constructive explorations, rather than just "messing around."

In demonstrating these behaviors, I work with the materials in our group lesson, showing them some ideas that they might try. For example, I examine objects carefully, arranging and displaying them in patterns and designs. I count objects by ones, twos, and fives. Even if they can't accomplish this, it sets the example of quiet, thoughtful work with a purpose.

After trying several activities, I ask the children to give me ideas for additional tasks using these materials, and then I model those suggestions. This way, even if the ideas are not completely constructive, I can take the opportunity to adapt them in order to troubleshoot for potentially off-task activity ahead of time.

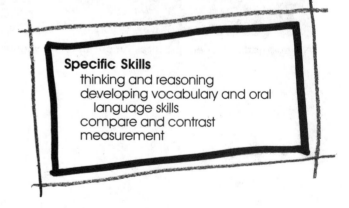

Specific Skills
thinking and reasoning
developing vocabulary and oral
    language skills
compare and contrast
measurement

Writing Math Story Problems

Create story problems having to do with a thematic unit or a book that the children read together, such as *The Magic School Bus Inside the Earth*, by Joanna Cole, or *The Doorbell Rang*, by Pat Hutchins.

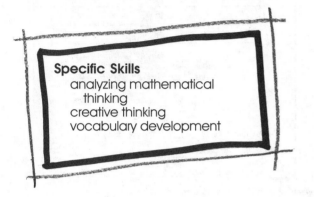

Specific Skills
analyzing mathematical
    thinking
creative thinking
vocabulary development

Counting Money

◎ Place sticky-back velcro onto coins so that real money can be used on a velcro board in centers. (You can find the looped side of velcro in fabric stores, or you may be able to obtain scraps from an automobile upholsterer.) Staple the velcro cloth to a flannel or cork board.

◎ Place money inside several plastic Ziploc™ bags. Ask the students to count the money in each bag and record it on paper.

Ⓜ Modify this task for different levels by adding story problems to the bags which require the students to make change, adding and subtracting the money in the bag.

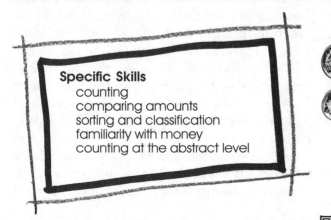

Specific Skills
counting
comparing amounts
sorting and classification
familiarity with money
counting at the abstract level

SUGGESTED MATERIALS

◎ charts for ongoing assessments and documentation of task completion (see Chapter 5).
◎ large shelf for manipulatives
◎ additional shelving for specific jobs (I have a separate shelf for my <u>Math Their Way</u> tubs)
◎ chalkboard or dry-wipe marker board (chalk and/or markers)
◎ large bulletin board for calendar and calendar math activities
◎ small tables or desks for completing tasks
◎ rug area for extended work on the floor
◎ Unifix™ cubes, Cuisenaire™ rods, links, chips, beads, and other manipulatives of your choice
◎ balance scales
◎ baskets or clear plastic tubs for holding math manipulatives
◎ graphing materials
◎ large and small abacus (counting frame)
◎ hundreds charts: cardboard model and pocket chart for children to use
◎ odd assortment of objects for sorting and classifying
◎ math and number games and puzzles
◎ chart stand for math charts, songs, and poems
◎ math-related literature books
◎ a manipulative program, such as <u>Math Their Way</u> or <u>Box It, Bag It</u> (Training for both are available throughout the country.)

Graphing Activities

m & m® Graph

Read and discuss the book, *The m & m's® Counting Book.* Allow your students to help you complete some of the number activities suggested in the book. Introduce the graphing activity by completing an enlarged version of the graph (use the copy machine to blow it up to 11" x 17").

Leave the graph in the math center as a task each child must do. As each child chooses this job, give him or her a small cup of m & m's to graph. Allow the children to eat their candy when their work is completed and checked. (This task could be included during a unit on colors or light and the color spectrum.)

Specific Skills
- counting
- invariance of number
- relationships between quantities
- patterns
- logical thinking

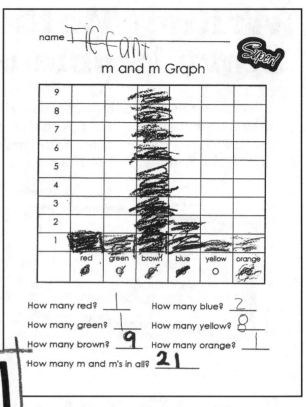

(Reproducibles on pages 184 and 185)

Rock Graph

Name _____

rock	1	2	3	4	5	6
white						
gray						
black						
brown						
red						
two colors						
three colors						
four colors						
five colors						

Graphing Rocks

This activity is a great one for building a sense of community in your classroom. It may be used in conjunction with a variety of thematic units, such as communities, fossils or earth science, or the Southwest United States.

Read the book, *Everybody Needs a Rock,* by Byrd Baylor. After a discussion on the book, take your class outside on a rock hunt. Have each child find a good rock "friend." Return to the classroom and complete a large edition of the total group graph, "My Rock" (reproducible on page 185 — the chart may have to be reproduced more than once and spliced together to make enough lines for your class).

Have each child draw a picture of his or her rock on the graph in the appropriate cell. Have crayons available to use that correspond to the colors of the rocks found by the children. After completing the graph, have the students write in their math journals, describing this activity and discussing the relationships between math and language and everyday life experiences.

Place small versions of the Rock Graph form in the math center along with a small basket of rocks. Ask each child to complete an individual graph when working in the math center. Point out to the children that their rock graphs will be different than the class graph. Discuss these differences.

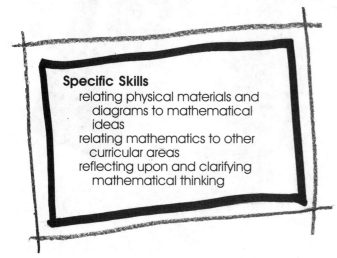

Specific Skills
relating physical materials and
    diagrams to mathematical
    ideas
relating mathematics to other
    curricular areas
reflecting upon and clarifying
    mathematical thinking

Graphing Related to Thematic Unit

Large graphs can be easily made with rolls of paper used to back bulletin boards. Simply run colored cloth tape across and down to form the cells of the graphs. Placing numbers across one side only will leave the graph open for graphing a variety of items. Laminating the empty graph allows you to place items on the graph with tape, and replace them without hurting the graph.

The same graph can be made using a plain plastic tablecloth or vinyl cloth, available at many large fabric shops. These can be hung in the math center or used on the floor during group lessons, then rolled for easy storage.

Examples of items to use for large graphing experiences according to thematic units include:

- types of shells found in a tub of sand in the center
- the children's favorite animals (during a unit on living things or animals)
- favorite fruits or vegetables, snack foods
- favorite learning centers
- fossils found on a field trip, or fossils made with plaster of Paris and natural items, such as shells, insects, and leaves. This can be tied into a natural history unit, studying dinosaurs and prehistoric history.

(M) Modify this task for different levels by changing the content of the graph from favorite animals to types of animals, such as mammals, reptiles, etc; or to natural habitats, such as air/land/water animals, or on what continent the animals are found.

(M) Another modification for different levels would be to create graphs of the five food groups, or to graph how the food groups help your body (providing energy, good for your muscles, good for your bones, etc.). Try a variety of graphs, such as circle, line, and/or line plot graphs.

Along with large class graphs, smaller graphs made on paper can be placed in the math center for students to complete as a must-do task. These enable you to assess each child's ability to make a graph and interpret it, as they answer questions about what information it gives.

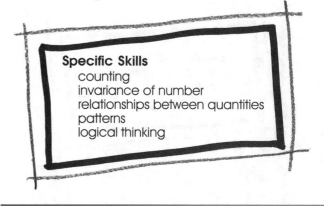

Specific Skills
counting
invariance of number
relationships between quantities
patterns
logical thinking

Extend and Create Patterns

Place paper cut-outs in the math center for extending and creating individual patterns. These can be generic, such as paper squares in a variety of colors, or they can be specific to a theme, such as paper flowers or animal stickers.

Specific Skills
extending and creating patterns
divergent thinking
analyzing patterns
left to right progression

Seriation of Materials

Place sets of bottles of colored water, sand, dried beans or peas, or coffee grounds in the math center. Each bottle within each set should contain a different amount of material. Ask the students to place the bottles in order, from least full to most full.

Specific Skills
seriation/ordering
comparing
measuring

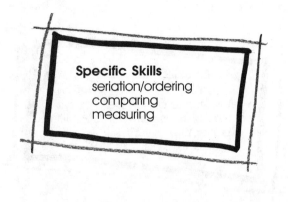

Math Journals

Many articles and books discuss the importance of having students write about their thinking process in their math problem solving. Keeping multiple journals can become overwhelming for the teacher and overkill for the students. However, mathematical thinking is an important skill which must be repeatedly practiced in order to be developed. I highly recommend that the teachers in your school investigate how to use math journals in your classrooms, and begin doing it as a group. Trying it as a group will encourage you to continue it, as you support each other with advice about what works well and what doesn't.

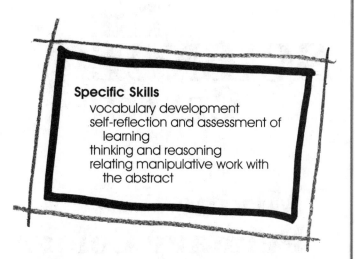

Specific Skills
vocabulary development
self-reflection and assessment of learning
thinking and reasoning
relating manipulative work with the abstract

Begin by having the children write in their math journals each day after they complete an activity at the end of a mini-lesson on a specific math skill. The children can keep their journals in the math center, so that they can write additional entries after working in the center.

This also provides an easy opportunity for you to conference with a student (or small group of students) if you notice a need for help in a particular area. You can review their journal entries and reteach the skill, then watch as they apply the skill in their work. Have them write another journal entry to reflect upon the changes they see in their understanding.

Explain math concepts (addition, subtraction, multiplication, and/or division) in words. When working in the center, have the children write in their math journals about a specific class problem that uses one of the concepts. Tell them to be specific in their explanation of what they do to solve the problem. (They might wish to use manipulatives to solve the problem, then draw a picture of what they did, then write about the picture.)

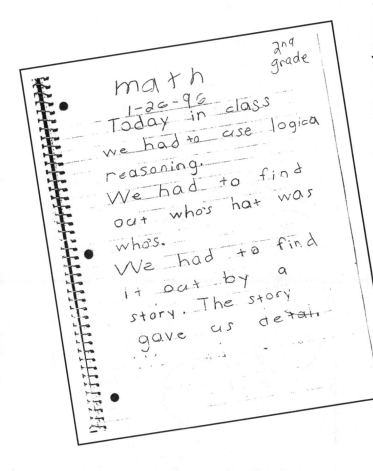

THE SCIENCE CENTER

Mixing Primary Colors

Give opportunities for mixing primary colors by providing these materials in the center:

Colored icing on graham crackers:
• Mix vanilla icing with food coloring to provide the three primary colors.
• Place icing, graham crackers, tongue depressors for spreading, and directions in the center.
• Each child may mix and spread icing to get a variety of colors.

Jello or finger paint in plastic bags:
• Place two primary colors in each bag.
• Secure opening of bags with masking tape.
• Each bag may be squished and mushed to see the mixing of the colors.

Eyedroppers and colored water:
• Place three jars of colored water (food coloring and water). Use primary colors (red, blue, and yellow).
• Provide an eyedropper for each jar.
• Allow the children to drip colored water onto soft paper towels or coffee filters, seeing how the colors mix.

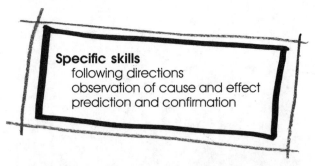

Specific skills
following directions
observation of cause and effect
prediction and confirmation

Create a Color Wheel

Teacher Preparation:

1. Mix primary colors (red, yellow, and blue) in three separate baby food jars by combining food coloring and water.

2. Create a color wheel on tagboard identical to the one in the diagram below.

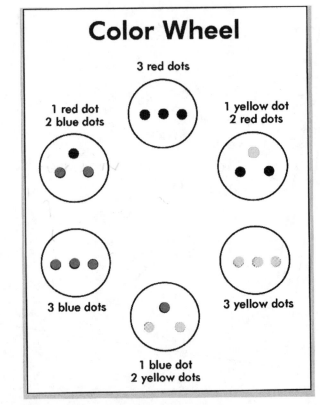

Color Wheel

3 red dots

1 red dot
2 blue dots

1 yellow dot
2 red dots

3 blue dots

3 yellow dots

1 blue dot
2 yellow dots

3. Laminate or cover with clear plastic contact paper.

4. Place the three baby food jars with the colored water on a tray in the learning center along with three eye-droppers, absorbent white paper towels, a toothpick, a pencil, and the laminated color wheel.

The Activity:

1. Demonstrate to the child how to drop colored water onto the colors of the laminated color wheel. Mix each puddle of colored water with the toothpick.

2. Write the child's name on a paper towel. Lay the towel over the laminated color wheel which contains the dots of colored water. Watch as the towel soaks up the water. The color wheel will appear on the towel.

3. Back the resulting color wheels with construction paper once they dry, if desired. The children can then write "color wheel" on the top of the paper.

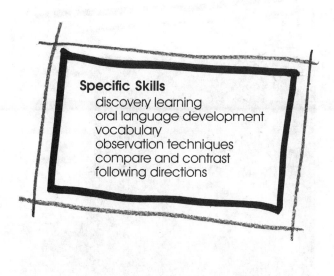

Specific Skills
discovery learning
oral language development
vocabulary
observation techniques
compare and contrast
following directions

- ▣ shelf with a large surface for displaying activities
- ▣ large table for extended work space
- ▣ small tables or desks to allow quiet space for individual investigations
- ▣ bookshelf for holding nonfiction books about specific topics
- ▣ windows, to tie science in with actual events just outside their window
- ▣ binoculars and clipboards hanging by the window to record sightings of birds, squirrels, changes in trees, etc.
- ▣ chart stands and board space for charts, posters, graphs, and pictures
- ▣ poetry charts, interactive charts, graphs, and posters for thematic units
- ▣ kitty litter box or sensory (water/sand) tables
- ▣ a computer with a CD-ROM encyclopedia for further study and independent investigations
- ▣ pets; books, charts, and graphs about the growth and care of these animals
- ▣ balance scales
- ▣ magnifying glasses
- ▣ stop watch or small clock with sweep second hand for timing experiments
- ▣ sand timers and kitchen timers
- ▣ trays for holding tasks carried from the shelf to the work tables
- ▣ a selection of science textbooks at various reading levels
- ▣ a selection of scoops, measuring spoons and cups, pitchers, funnels of different sizes, sifters, water pumps, magnets, manipulatives for self-discovery
- ▣ indoor/outdoor thermometer; weather graph
- ▣ tasks and materials specific to each unit
- ▣ plants: seeds (avocado), roots and tubers (sweet potato), and bulbs
- ▣ planters with glass or clear plastic sides for observing root development
- ▣ hand towels for cleaning up spills (sink and float, water table)

Recording the Temperature

Place an indoor/outdoor thermometer in a window near the science center. Keep a class graph of the temperature, with columns for recording both indoor and outdoor readings. When students work in the science center, it is their responsibility to check and record the temperatures onto the graph.

Ⓜ Modify this task for different levels by asking additional activities, such as:

- having the students make individual bar graphs at the end of each month, answering questions by interpreting the graph
- predicting what the average temperature will be next month
- figuring the average difference between the indoor and outdoor temperature

Specific Skills
  following directions
  measurement
  graphing skills
  counting
  observational skills
  patterns
  prediction

Measurement and Conservation

Place a measuring cup and clear plastic containers of different widths in the sand table along with dried beans, corn, or peas. Put rubber bands around the containers.

On sentence strips or a poster, print the following directions for the students to follow:

1. Measure 2 cups of beans.
2. Predict how high the beans will fill one container. Move the rubber band to that spot around the container.
3. Pour the beans into the container. Was your prediction close?
4. Try again with a new container.

Specific Skills
  measurement
  conservation
  following directions
  prediction
  beginning abstract thinking
  compare and contrast

Science Observation

Place an item in your science center that is tied in some way to your thematic unit. For example, you might use:

- a fossil during a unit on earth science or dinosaurs
- a natural sponge during an ocean unit
- a seed pod during a unit on living things or plants
- a tadpole or caterpillar during a unit on changes

Model how to examine something as a scientist would, noticing every detail, taking notes and drawings, finding precise words to describe it. Introduce the microscope and the hand lens as tools that enable the scientist to observe details. List new vocabulary words the children give orally on a chart to place in the center. Ask a student to draw a picture of the object as the class notices details that should be included. Write a paragraph describing the item on a chart or board, using words generated from the list created by the children.

Show the children the observation form and explain that you would like them to be the scientist, using drawings and words to describe the object you have placed in the center. Provide drawing pencils, colored pencils, fine colored markers, large erasers, and whatever other tools the students suggest they might need.

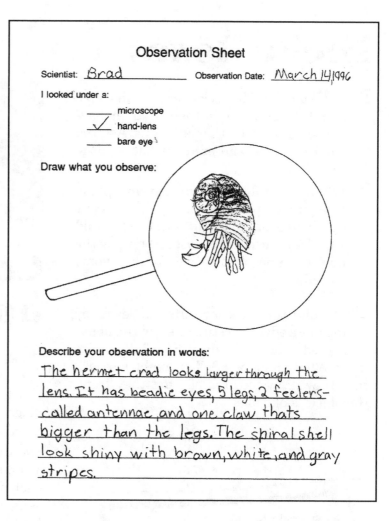

Observation Sheet

Scientist: _Brad_   Observation Date: _March 14, 1996_

I looked under a:

_____ microscope
__✓__ hand-lens
_____ bare eye

Draw what you observe:

Describe your observation in words:

The hermet crad looks larger through the lens. It has beadie eyes, 5 legs, 2 feelers-called antennae, and one claw thats bigger than the legs. The spiral shell look shiny with brown, white, and gray stripes.

(Reproducible on page 186)

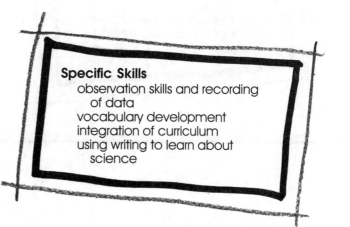

Specific Skills
observation skills and recording
  of data
vocabulary development
integration of curriculum
using writing to learn about
  science

Feelie Boxes

◎ Place a large tube sock over a small coffee can. Put an object in the container having to do with the thematic unit. Ask the children to feel and predict what is in the can.

◎ When all children have had an opportunity to complete this task, pull the object out during a total group period. The child who drew the picture most resembling the object can be given the can to take home to refill.

Ⓜ Modify this task for different levels by asking more advanced students to write about their predictions: How does it feel? What size is it? What shape is it? You might also ask that they draw pictures of what they think the object looks like.

Specific Skills
creative thinking
observation through senses
vocabulary
oral language development
beginning abstract thinking
logical thinking

Compare and Contrast

Place two items on a tray with a magnifying glass, pencils, colored pencils or markers, measuring tape and ruler, scale, and Venn diagram sheets.

Model how to compare and contrast the two items, recording the comparisons on the Venn diagram. Demonstrate how to examine each item in a variety of ways, using the senses, the magnifying glass, a measuring tape or ruler, scale, etc.

Ⓜ Modify this task for different levels by requiring more writing, describing each item in detail. Some suggested items might include:

a hermit crab and a gerbil
a fossil and a stone
an acorn and a pine cone
a ramp and a pulley

Specific Skills
observational techniques and skills
recording data
following directions
compare and contrast
creative thinking strategies

Examining Bones

◩ Collect old bones from your ham, turkey, and chicken dinners. Boil them and lay them out to dry for several days. When a good collection has been assembled, take them to school for your natural history unit. Place them in a tub, kitty litter box, or sand table. Let the students investigate them, predicting what animal they are from.

◩ Read books about dinosaur fossils and bones, such as *Bones, Bones, Dinosaur Bones,* by Byron Barton, or *My Visit to the Dinosaurs,* by Aliki. Model how to investigate the bones, showing how to:

- dig up bones placed in dirt or sand in the sand table (provide paintbrushes to uncover the bones, just as archaeologists do)

- weigh the bones

- classify the bones by what animal they came from or by similar shape

- draw and write about the bones found

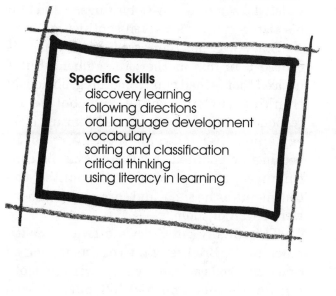

Specific Skills
discovery learning
following directions
oral language development
vocabulary
sorting and classification
critical thinking
using literacy in learning

Writing in Science

◩ List science-related vocabulary used in thematic units, or in science generally (such as *hypothesis, predict,* etc.), on a chart in the center. Ask students to choose from these words when writing in their thematic journals.

◩ Have students use these words in their writing activities within the science center, or in cooperative projects. Students can add new words to the list as they investigate a topic or as the class begins new units.

m Modify this task for different levels by creating a class science dictionary, having each student choose a new word to add during each thematic unit.

Specific Skills
vocabulary development
reflective writing
alphabetical order

The Geography Center

Teaching Geography

Whenever I give presentations and in-services, my geography materials get the most attention from teachers. Because this center is unique to the primary classroom, and I believe the activities themselves are unique to even intermediate classrooms, it might be helpful if I explain in some detail how I go about teaching the concepts I promote in this center. It is one of my favorite areas of the curriculum, and is always a favorite of my students and their parents. But first, let me explain how it all started.

I began including geography in my classroom about eight years ago, when my son attended Children's Meeting House, a Montessori school in Loveland, Ohio. One evening my oldest daughter, who was in fourth grade at the time, was completing a homework sheet on world geography. Stacy was filling in the names of the seven continents and felt sure that her teacher had made a mistake. She could only locate six of them, and she was very frustrated. I was stumped, too; this was the first time I had been asked by my children for help with their homework, and I was more lost than they were!

Stacy was complaining and near tears, when her three-year-old brother walked through the room. Brad adored his oldest sister, and stopped to ask her if he could help. (If you've ever had a female fourth grader in your home, you can imagine her response. If you haven't, you shouldn't try. It was ugly.) She admonished her little brother for thinking he would know how many continents there were, then continued her moaning and groaning. Now, her little brother, who was no higher than her waist, did something with his fingers, and told his sister there were seven continents.

Stacy was not impressed, but I was. (Of course I am his mother, remember.) But I noticed that he had done something, obviously thinking through something, before he responded to her. I questioned him until he explained that he knew there were seven because he counted them! He sang his continent song from school and counted the continents as he sang, and sure enough, there were seven of them!

This finally got Stacy's attention. With much pride, Brad sang the continent song as Stacy checked each one she had written, looking for the one she had left out. (It was Antarctica.) As Brad grew about three inches, I saw the power he felt with this knowledge.

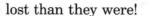

At the age of three, he knew more than his mother and sister. Usually a very shy child, he was anxious to return to school the next day! It was at that moment that I decided I needed to begin teaching geography.

The teachers at his school were very supportive, and offered books and advice on Maria Montessori's philosophy of teaching geography to young children. I was also fortunate to be teaching with a wonderful teacher, Judith Penry, who was getting her Master's degree in Montessori Education at the time. With all their advice, I managed to put together my program.

As I mentioned earlier, the geography center began as a part of my science center, but has held its own ever since. I cannot explain what this has done for my teaching. The sense of community in our classroom and the interest and understanding the children show about other cultures are amazing. When my young students come back to school after explaining something about their study of geography to their parents, I always know it. They are so anxious to learn! They know they are smart, and they feel so strong. And the lesson they reteach me every year is clear: Never underestimate the intelligence of a child.

I believe that you can teach young children just about anything if you do it in the right way. It's all in the process. Break the information down to the simplest form, then let them experience it in some way. Surround them with pictures. Read them books. Feed them new foods. Tell them stories. Teach them to sing the language. Fill their minds with ideas of people and places and families, and they can understand a lot about the whole, wide world.

Beginning the Year With Geography

I begin the year with six to eight weeks of instruction about what geography is all about. We learn about physical geography first. We look at globes, and giggle that our world is round, when we can look out our window and see that it is perfectly flat out there! So we go outside and we put our hands around a small ball, and feel how our fingers wrap around it. Next we try this with a tennis ball, then a small playground ball, then a basketball. Oh my! What is happening to our curved hand? Then we lay

our hands on a very large ball or balloon, and see that our hands lie flat against its surface. Finally, we all place our hands flat against the ground, and feel the largest ball of all, the planet earth. Wow. You can almost see the children spinning with the recognition that they're sitting on this rotating planet. They touch it for a long time, almost patting it as though they sense that they should take very good care of it.

The next lesson involves a clay ball. I use hard clay with another color mixed in to create little spots, like continents on the surface of the earth. We look at the shapes of the continents on the globe and we compare them to the shapes on a flat map. Oh my! What has happened to Antarctica? This is strange. I cut the ball of clay in half and flatten the pieces out with my palm, in order to make a nice flat surface to carry in my pocket. The children see how distorted the spots of colored clay become as I flatten my two hemispheres.

We learn more about what maps are and what they tell us about the places they represent. We learn the song about the continents. It's a simple song. Make one up to any familiar tune. Just begin with North America, and work your way around the planet, left to right:

South America, Africa, Europe, Asia, Australia, Antarctica. (See, there really are seven!)

I then move on in my curriculum to political geography. We usually spend about a month on each continent, visiting North America twice. We learn about Mexico as well as the United States. We bring in everything we can that will tell us more about the places we learn about — visitors, parents, grandparents, books, flags, toys, musical instruments, clothing, money, animals, languages, songs, stories, crafts, and anything else that helps us understand other areas of the world.

If I taught older students, I think I'd begin my geography the same way, because they have probably never been exposed to much of the world. They'll probably move more rapidly through the fundamentals, but that is where I would begin.

Stocking Your Geography Center

To stock your center, ask parents for postcards, old *National Geographic* magazines for pictures, odd foreign coins, and any information they can provide. Visit shops that specialize in foreign trinkets. Ask friends and relatives who travel to send postcards and stamps, and bring home money and little toys from that country. (A friend of mine went around the world and sent me a card filled with stamps from all over the world!)

Call travel agencies and ask for old posters and booklets on travel. You will acquire more than you need in no time at all.

In teaching about the cultures and traditions of faraway places, I rely on trade books. There is an abundance of quality children's literature to teach us about our world. Make certain the information is authentic. I like books that give me additional facts about the location and people, and offer background information on how the book was written. Look up countries in the encyclopedia to learn more.

Put a computer in your geography center. The children can use the encyclopedia on the CD-ROM or play the new CD-ROM version of "Where In the World Is Carmen Sandiego?" There are lots of materials out there that will help you adapt your center for your students' interests and ability level. Have fun!

THE GEOGRAPHY CENTER

Flags

We make our flags from half of a 9" x 12" piece of construction paper. I have all the strips of other colors precut, along with pieces of construction paper needed for designs on the flag. When shapes are needed, such as the star on the Chinese flag or the diamond and circle for Brazil, I place three cardboard stencils of the shapes in the geography center with the materials for the flags. The students may trace and cut the specific shapes themselves. (The smaller stars on the Chinese flag are punched with a star-shaped hole punch from the scraps around the larger star.)

For flags that involve emblems, such as Kenya and Mexico, I simply make a copy of the flag from an encyclopedia and blow it up until the emblem is the correct size for our flag. Then I make multiple copies of just the emblem for the children to cut out and place on their flag.

Cardboard strips approximately 1½" by 6" are also placed with the materials. The children staple or glue these to the back of the left side of their flag for the pole. I instruct them to write the name of the country on the flag pole so that they can recall the name of the country when they take it home. Many of my students save these all year and decorate their rooms at home with them.

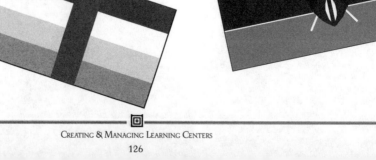

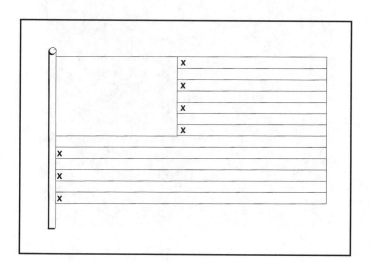

There are two exceptions to the flags my students make. Australia's flag is very difficult, so I make copies for the children to color. When we make our American flag, I make full 8 ½" x 11" copies of it. I cut thin strips of red for the children to paste onto the flag over every row that is marked with an "x", and a blue rectangle to paste onto the top left corner. Stars can be made using crayons or stickers. I do not make them attempt to place all 50 stars on correctly. (Reproducible flag patterns are on pages 187-190.)

Ⓜ Modify this task for different levels by learning about the symbolism of the flags, asking the students to write about what each color means, as well as the meanings of any shapes, stripes, or animals. This may be done in cooperative groups, or individually.

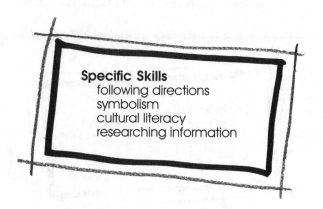

Specific Skills
following directions
symbolism
cultural literacy
researching information

Cultural Literature Books and Stories

Develop cultural literacy: Display (and read aloud) a wide variety of books from other countries in the geography center.

Encourage your students to retell the stories using flannel board characters, puppets, or storyboards. The students can organize their materials and practice retelling folktales and legends in the center, then ask to present one to the class at a later time.

Specific Skills
reading for enjoyment
story sense
comprehension skills
vocabulary development
cultural literacy
oral language development

Classification

1. Paint the lids of three baby food jars: one blue, one white, one brown. Have the children fill them: Leave the jar with the white lid empty to represent air; place earth in the jar with the brown lid; place water in the jar with the blue lid.

2. Make word cards from colored cardboard or matting board to match the jars:

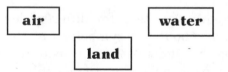

air		water
	land	

3. Sort pictures of places, animal shapes, or small transportation vehicles from around the world according to air, land, or water.

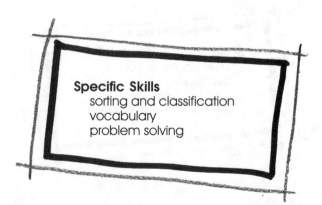

Specific Skills
sorting and classification
vocabulary
problem solving

Working With Maps

Make a map of the animals of South America:

Cut the shape of the continent out of large matting board. This becomes a stencil for the map. I use easel paper to make the maps, so the size of my stencil is just smaller than 18" x 24". Write the name of the continent on the board for the children to see. They can use this to copy the name of the continent, as well as knowing the map is positioned correctly when tracing the shape.

Make a worksheet showing pictures of animals you will discuss while learning about this continent. Simple pictures can be found in encyclopedias or animal encyclopedias. You might find animals that match books you have and pictures you have found from magazines such as *National Geographic, Ranger Rick, Big Back Yard,* and *World.* Put the pictures onto a worksheet and make a copy for each child.

Show the children how to cut out each animal and paste it onto the map they have traced. Young children are able to see that this is where these animals live, and that maps represent what the place is really like.

Make other maps depicting a variety of aspects such as:

- natural habitats of favorite animals
- endangered animals around the world
- tropical rain forests of the world
- mountain ranges of the world

Locate specific places on a map:

Write to schools in other parts of the country or world, depending on your curriculum. Ask questions about the students, and place a pin on a map whenever a letter is answered.

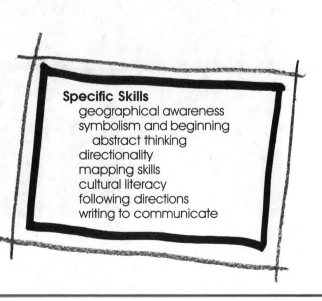 Modify this task for different levels by sending artwork, writing group letters to an entire class from your class, or asking that each student in your class write to a school in a different state or country. (Send letters or postcards to "A Fourth Grade Class, Local Elementary School, Give specific City and State," to have it delivered to a school in the state, or write the local chamber of commerce first to get the name of a school to write to.)

Specific Skills
geographical awareness
symbolism and beginning
   abstract thinking
directionality
mapping skills
cultural literacy
following directions
writing to communicate

Multicultural Crafts

Create art activities and craft projects that symbolize other cultures in your geography center. Some might include:

▣ Read *Dreamcatcher*, by Audrey Osofsky. Make a dreamcatcher using embroidery hoops or the outside of a paper plate, string, beads, and a feather.

▣ Read *The Whispering Cloth: A Refugee's Story*, by Pegi Deitz Shea. Using felt or burlap, large plastic needles, and yarn, have the students stitch a cloth (according to the ability of your students) that tells a story about them, or simply lets them make stitches in the cloth. Have them use this to tell their story to the class.

▣ Read *Grandfather Tang's Story*, by Ann Tompert. Cut a tangram for each child. Ask each child to create a shape from her paper tangram and tell a story about it. Cutting the shapes from brown paper and placing them on rice paper creates a nice texture to the story. You can also cut the tangrams from wallpaper scraps.

Cultural Artifacts for Play and Investigation

Place toys or musical instruments in the center that come from the country you are learning about.

⟲ Modify this activity for different levels by challenging advanced students to make games using the toys, or write songs using the instruments and a few words in the language of that country (such as a counting song, counting in the foreign language).

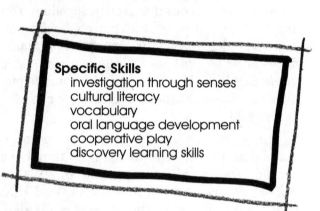

Specific Skills
investigation through senses
cultural literacy
vocabulary
oral language development
cooperative play
discovery learning skills

Tangram

(Reproducible on page 191)

Felt Continent Puzzle

◉ Cut continents from felt, each one a different color. Cover a board with blue felt. Draw two circles (hemispheres) onto the felt. Instruct the children how to recreate a world map by placing the felt continents onto the flannel board hemispheres.

◉ Have the children make a simple map of the world, coloring each continent the same color as the felt pieces.

◉ The continents may also be made from magnetic sheets to place on a dry-wipe board or chalkboard that is magnetic.*

Specific Skills
matching
following directions
physical geography
vocabulary
spatial perception

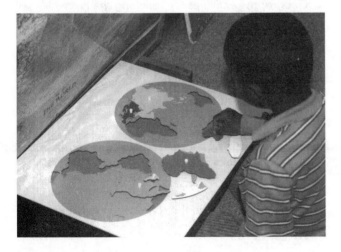

* Dies to cut the continents and tangram, as well as magnetic sheets, may be purchased from Ellison Press, 1-800-253-2238.

Bilingual Books and Learning Another Language

Place bilingual books in this center. Ask a high school foreign language student, exchange student, parent volunteer from this country, or foreign language teacher to record the story in the second language. Include books that have songs sung in the second language on the tape. Learn to sing a song in the language together as a class. Record it together to listen to in the center.

Specific Skills
cultural literacy
language development
vocabulary development
cooperative learning skills
oral language development

◙ Chapter 7 ◙

Teacher Resources in Math

Balka, Don. *Unifix Mathematics Activities: Book 1.* Peabody, MA: DIDAX Educational Resources, 1987.

Baratta-Lorton, Mary. *Mathematics Their Way.* Menlo Park, CA: Addison-Wesley, 1976.

———.*Workjobs II: Number Activities for Early Childhood.* Menlo Park, CA: Addison-Wesley, 1979.

Braddon, Kathryn L., Hall, Nancy J., and Taylor, Dale. *Math Through Children's Literature: Making the NCTM Standards Come Alive.* Englewood, CO: Teacher Ideas Press, 1993.

Teacher Resources in Science

Brainard, Audrey, and Wrubel, Denise H. *Literature-Based Science Activities.* New York: Scholastic, 1993.

Butzow, Carol M., and Butzow, John W. *Science Through Children's Literature.* Englewood, CO: Teacher Ideas Press, 1989.

Gates, Julie M. *Consider the Earth.* (environmental educational activities: Grades 4-8) Englewood, CO: Teacher Ideas Press, 1989.

Instructor Books, *Foolproof, Failsafe Seasonal Science.* New York: Instructor Books, 1982.

Kenda, Margaret, and Williams, Phyllis S. *Science Wizardry for Kids.* Hauppauge, NY: Barron's, 1992.

Lingelbach, Jenepher (Ed.). *Hands-On Nature.* Woodstock, VT: Vermont Institute of Natural Science, 1986.

Poppe, Carol A., and VanMatre, Nancy A. *Science Learning Centers for the Primary Grades.* West Nyack, NY: The Center for Applied Research in Education, 1985.

Rockwell, Robert E.; Sherwood, Elizabeth A.; and Williams, Robert A. *Hug a Tree.* Mt. Rainier, MD: Gryphon House, 1983.

Ruef, Kerry. *The Private Eye.* Seattle: The Private Eye Project, 1992.

Williams, Robert A.; Rockwell, Robert E.; and Sherwood, Elizabeth A. *Mudpies to Magnets.* Mt. Rainier, MD: Gryphon House, 1987.

Teacher Resources in Geography

Allen, Judy; McNeill, Earldene; and Schmidt, Velma. *Cultural Awareness for Children.* Menlo Park, CA: Addison-Wesley, 1992.

Boutte, G.S., and McCormick, C.B. "Authentic Multicultural Activities" *Childhood Education 68* (1992): 140-144.

Cech, M. *Globalchild: Multicultural Resources for Young Children.* Menlo Park, CA: Addison-Wesley, 1991.

Derman-Sparks, Louise and the A.B.C. Task Force, *Anti-Bias Curriculum,* Washington, D.C.: National Association for the Education of Young Children, 1989.

Enciso, Patricia. "Integrating Cultural Imagination" *The Reading Teacher 47* (1993/1994): 336-337.

Farrell, Catharine. *Storytelling in Our Multicultural World.* (storytelling kits with stories, lesson plans, activities, and manipulatives) Columbus, OH: Zaner-Bloser, 1995.

Gomez, Aurelia. *Crafts of Many Cultures.* New York: Scholastic, 1992.

Graham, Leland, and Brandon, Traci. *A Trip Around the World* (Grades K-3). Greensboro, NC: Carson-Dellosa, 1993.

Grevious, Saundrah Clark. *Ready-to-Use Multicultural Activities for Primary Children.* West Nyack, NY: Center for Applied Research in Education, 1993.

Massachusetts Geographic Alliance. *Global Geography: Activities for Teaching the Five Themes of Geography.* (Grades 3-9) Boulder, CO: Social Science Education Consortium, 1990.

McCarthy, Tara. *Literature-Based Geography Activities.* New York: Scholastic, 1992.

Montessori, Maria M. *Childhood Education.* New York: Meridian, 1949.

Seldin, Tim, and Raymond, Donna. *Geography and History for the Young Child.* (The Montessori Approach) Provo, UT: Brigham Young University Press, 1981.

Williams, L.R., and Degaetano, Y. *ALERTA: A Multicultural, Bilingual Approach to Teaching Young Children.* Menlo Park, CA: Addison-Wesley, 1985.

Children's Trade Books From This Chapter

Aliki. *My Visit to the Dinosaurs*. New York: Harper and Row, 1985.

Barton, Byron. *Bones, Bones, Dinosaur Bones*. New York: HarperCollins, 1990.

Baylor, Byrd. *Everybody Needs a Rock*. New York: Aladdin, 1974.

Cannon, Janell. *Stellaluna*, New York: Harcourt Brace, 1993.

Cole, Joanna. *The Magic School Bus Lost in the Solar System*. New York: Scholastic, 1990.

Earle, Ann. *Zipping, Zapping, Zooming Bats*. New York: HarperCollins, 1995.

Hutchins, Pat. *The Doorbell Rang*. New York: Greenwillow Books, 1986.

McGrath, Barbara Barbieri. *The m & m's® Counting Book*. Watertown, MA: Charlesbridge Publishing, 1994.

Osofsky, Audrey. *Dreamcatcher*. New York: Orchard Books, 1992.

Shea, Pegi Deitz. *The Whispering Cloth: A Refugee's Story*. Honesdale, PA: Boyds Mills Press, 1995.

Tompert, Ann. *Grandfather Tang's Story*. New York: Crown, 1990.

Other Resources Mentioned in This Chapter:

Where in the World Is Carmen Sandiego? CD-ROM game

Compton's Interactive Encyclopedia. Compton's New Media © 1994,1995.

Resources for Products:

Delta Education
P.O. Box 3000
Nashua, NH 03061-3000
1-800-442-5444

Delta is an excellent source for creative manipulatives for science and math. Their catalog has a wide selection of good teacher resource books, as well.

The Ellison Press Co.
P.O. Box 8209
Newport Beach, CA 92658
1-800-253-2238

Dies for continents, tangrams, and magnetic sheets.

Hero Arts

A set of continent rubber stamps manufactured by Hero Arts is available at most stores where other stamps may be purchased, such as children's bookstores or card stores.

Nienhuis Montessori USA
320 Pioneer Way
Mountain View, CA 94041-1576
1-800-942-8697

Nienhuis materials are exceptional. I purchased the globe and wooden puzzle map from them. My geography center would not be the same without them.

Zaner-Bloser, Inc.
P.O. Box 16764
Columbus, OH 43216-6764
1-800-421-3018

Storytelling kits, complete with stories from a variety of cultures, props, teacher's resource guide, audiotapes, and story cards. Four separate kits: *Family Tales*, *Animal Tales*, *Neighborhood Tales*, and *Pot Full of Tales*.

Creative Development Centers

"When I grow up," I tell her, "I too will go to faraway places and come home to live by the sea."

"That is all very well, little Alice," says my aunt, "but there is a third thing you must do."

"What is that?" I ask.

"You must do something to make the world more beautiful."

"All right," I say.

— Barbara Cooney,
Miss Rumphius

In my classroom, we spend time creating lots of things: We write poems and songs, we paint at the easel, we create fiction and nonfiction books, we mix foods together to taste something new, we draw people and places and things. In short, we make a lot of messes. But they are creative messes. As my children create their masterpieces, they learn to take risks, to see things from another perspective, to learn from trying again and again and again.

Thinking creatively is part of every activity. I often introduce a new task by asking my students what they think we might do with the materials. I like them to think for themselves, but we have to show them how to do that, as well as letting them know it's okay. Often, children are used to waiting to be told just what to do, and they're admonished if they jump in to offer explanations too early. When I ask them to tell me what we could do with this stuff, I let them know that I trust them to think for themselves and will accept their views. This helps them feel safe to be creative and think individually, rather than spending time wondering what the teacher wants them to say or do.

In my creative development centers, the children learn to take risks, to enjoy adventure, to experience making mistakes and figuring out how to correct them, to use materials creatively, and to accept their best work as a great creation. They have opportunities to talk through this process, and to share ideas and listen to other perspectives. They experience hearing others give opinions about their work, and make their own decisions about what to do with that advice.

This area of the classroom needs lots of work space, lots of storage places, and plenty of room to move about. It's an active area that shouldn't be stifled by limitations.

The Art Task Table

I have two tables in my art center. The first is used to nurture skills needed in order to work creatively: fine motor development, following directions, using basic shapes and patterns, and using color and space effectively. At this table, the children create art projects independently, following directions I have given them. They do not have a model to duplicate in front of them; they are encouraged to make creative decisions on their own, designing their own masterpiece within the guidelines of the project. These projects are usually related to our thematic unit in some way.

The Day/Night Book

My curriculum states that, when learning about the solar system, my children should be able to verbalize the difference between day and night. At this art table, we make a day/night book. We divide a large piece of construction paper into two sides. We make a moon and a sun from yellow paper, and the children write the words "day" and "night" at the top of their papers. Then they create two pictures, one showing what they like to do during the day, the other what they enjoy doing during the night.

Sometimes we color with crayons, sometimes we use torn paper scraps. The project changes as the children show an interest or a need in one area or another. When the children have all completed their pictures, they

The Day/Night Book (lower left) and other books created by my students.

tell me long-winded stories about their adventures, while I take dictation. (By this time in the year, they are very talkative.) We put the pictures and stories together to make a class book, and it is always a favorite.

While the children are in art creating their masterpiece, they are gaining a better understanding of the difference between day and night, writing the words and associating them to their life, reflecting upon their experiences, using their fine motor skills, and using vocabulary and oral language.

The Independent Art Table

crayons

The second table is much messier and has fewer guidelines. It has materials that rotate in and out of the station, giving children opportunities to create whatever they wish. Fingerpaint, colored chalk, paper scraps, pieces of material scraps, hole punches of various shapes, and playdough are put out for the children throughout the year for them to experiment with. I often model the use of the materials, as well as instructing how to make something fit around one's head, or how to tear paper into shapes rather than cut it. At this table, the work is not usually tied to the thematic unit, for I don't assign a specific task to complete. My main goal is for the children to think creatively with materials, use oral language skills and fine motor control, and explain what they have made and how they accomplished it. They might choose to create something that ties in with our unit, but it isn't mandatory.

When working in the art center, my students work at both tables, completing the art task as well as experimenting with the materials to create something of their own design at the second table. They can choose which table to work at first, but both jobs must get done before they move to another center.

The Easel

My easel is a separate center, as I explained in Chapter 2. I have a double easel, so that the spaces on one side of the easel are used for a specific, assigned activity and the spaces on the other side are used as another choice activity. My students complete both activities before their work at the easel is finished.

The materials on the second side of the easel are different than on the first, so that not only do my children work at two separate tasks, they use different materials while completing them. These materials change about every two weeks, after each child has had an opportunity to complete the assignment. This runs much the same as our two art tables.

A kindergartner begins a work of art.

For example, when we went to the zoo, we came back to the room and mixed paint to come up with some really earthy colors. The children chose their favorite animal from the zoo to paint, and had to use invented spelling to write its name on the paper. On the opposite side of the easel, I put large crayons with colored paper, and they could design anything they liked. Many chose to draw the entire zoo, for using crayons allowed them to add more detail than did the paints on the other side.

Another time, during our unit on weather and the seasons, we used crayons to color a picture of ourselves enjoying our favorite season. The children had to copy the name of the season onto the paper (copy, because I was building their vocabulary, and so I wanted them to see and write it correctly). Later in the writing center, they used these papers to create a poetry book, writing three rhyming words that described their season. With this project, the children practiced their handwriting, gave detailed information through drawing, and practiced expressing an idea. I was able to assess their ability to give rhyming sounds as they told me their three descriptive words.

On the opposite side of the easel, we put colored chalk on dark paper. Again, they could do whatever they liked at the second side. The idea was to be creative with another medium.

In classrooms with older students, I have seen an easel used in a rotating creative arts center. While sometimes the children create their own projects at a table, on other occasions the table is replaced by an easel, and they are free to create a masterpiece there. It is a nice way to find time with older children to continue to nurture the physical skills and creative thinking that these activities promote.

Again, choose a variety of materials for them to use at the easel. Easels aren't just for painting. You might ask them which they prefer to use for specific projects. Taking ownership will encourage them to do their best when they go to complete the task.

You can see that each project my students are asked to complete is designed to nurture their creativity, their physical development, and their social/emotional development, as well as make connections between their creative thinking and the concepts we are learning about in the current thematic unit. All of these areas are considered when I design projects for them in our creative centers. I avoid using projects that are simply cute or are merely time fillers. If you want your students to give you quality work, you must make their work meaningful.

A Research Center

I have also included information on a research center you might wish to consider. It can be introduced as part of another center or a temporary center, before giving it permanent space in your classroom.

It can be included in almost any center. I like to emphasize the creative element that research offers the student, rather than the obvious link to the cognitive domain. Introducing young learners to the process of research invites them to take control of the learning process in a completely new way. It is, for me, a powerful demonstration of how to use my knowledge and intelligence in a creative way to change what I do. At this stage of learning about research, that is what I want to emphasize most.

Even kindergartners can be guided through the process of designing their own research projects, but to work independently at them in a center, I would advise your students be at least eight or nine years old. I have seen research centers as part of a science center in a kindergarten classroom, but I would not recommend this practice. There is so much investigation to do with manipulatives in science, that I don't think young children need to regularly spend their time with organized research during their center activities. I don't want to modify the intent or process so much that I miseducate my students, having them believe that research is something it isn't.

A Note About Computers

There are many ways to include computers in your learning centers. I have taught in a classroom that had a computer right in the room; it was great! I tried it in a variety of different centers, using programs suited to the topics of each center.

For example, I put the computer in the math center with programs that enriched or provided practice for skills I was covering. Then, I moved it to the science center, including a computer game based on Mrs. Frizzle's field trips (from Scholastic's *Magic School Bus* series) that matched a thematic unit I was doing at the time. When the children began writing sentences in their journals, the computer showed up in the writing center. This gave children opportunities to begin learning how to revise and edit their writing.

Because I only had one computer, I often kept it in the games center, where children were allowed to use any program they wanted to use. In this center, I did not limit the computer's use to one topic or one area of the curriculum.

Be Creative

It's important to be creative with the resources available to you. If you only have one computer, move it around to provide a variety of experiences for your students. If you do have more than one computer in your classroom, try to use them throughout the room, rather than pulling them together into one area of the classroom. After all, we want our students to become accustomed to using computers in all aspects of their life and work. This can best be accomplished by including a computer in every learning center.

Math computers can be used for practicing skills, completing math journals, and playing games related to logical thinking, statistics, patterning, graphing, classification, and spatial relationships. In the science center, students can use the computer to keep data on a spreadsheet, explore the universe through the Internet, and discover chemistry through virtual labs.

Geography computers can link a student with an international pen pal via electronic mail. Recipes can be kept, revised, and adapted to single servings or large crowds on a computer in a cooking center. Writing or publishing centers can use computers to take children through the entire writing process, allowing each student to publish professional-quality books independently.

Children can write to their favorite authors or illustrators via e-mail, as well as having access to the great libraries, museums, and art galleries of the world. Imagine taking a virtual field trip through the Louvre! Students can create their own music on the computer, without having to play a single instrument. They can combine colors and use a variety of media without making a mess!

We have no idea how our children will use computers in the future, for the technology is changing daily. The possibilities are endless, which is exactly the lesson you want to get across with computers.

Back to Reality — The Computer Lab

Now that I've had fun creating the perfect environment for computers in a learning-center-based classroom, I should come back to reality; otherwise I will be completely depressed when I go into my classroom tomorrow.

What do you do when — like me — all you have is thirty minutes a day in the computer lab down the hall? I have found a way that works very well for my students. It gives us a little more flexibility with how we use our computer time, and provides some feeling of choice for the students.

I include our computer lab on our center chart; each day, my students know that they can choose to go to the computer center anytime after ten o'clock. They may ask to take their writing folder and revise some writing, or they may wish to make a birthday card for a family member. Others may choose to play a computer game I have chosen that goes with our thematic unit.

As teachers, we are used to making do with the resources we are given; this is the honest reality of life in the public school systems. While thirty minutes in a computer lab down the hall isn't as exciting as the classroom filled with computers that I created in my mind, it does give some sense of empowerment to the children and offers many ways of using computers as they do their work. It makes them *comfortable* with the concept of using computers as a powerful, multipurpose tool throughout their lives, which is the point.

THE ART CENTER

Musical Instruments

Murals

Create a mural of the zoo, an ocean, a tropical rain forest, or a farm using a variety of art media, such as finger painting and tissue paper collage. Utilize a bulletin board or an entire corner of the room. Hang streamers from the ceiling for vines, build trees up the wall with large paper bags stuffed with old newspapers. Make rocks or coconuts from stuffed paper bags. Fill the space with objects. Ask the children for suggestions. Add to it little by little as children work in the art center.

Specific Skills
- fine motor control
- applying knowledge
- cooperative work strategies
- creative thinking
- reading for information

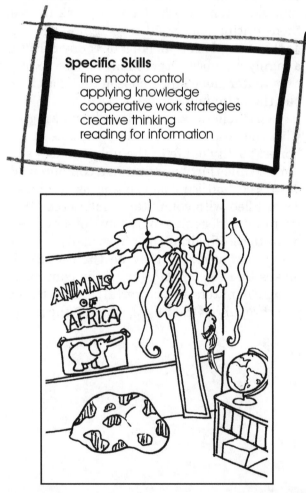

Make a variety of musical instruments with various materials. Create a music store where students can buy the instruments. Write ads for them and display them around the school. Create music to use with the instruments and form a band.

Some suggested instruments and the materials to use might include:

- a drum from an empty can with ends cut from a paper grocery bag; put dried rice, corn or beans in the can to make a different shaker sound.
- maracas from empty film canisters filled with dried beans, rice, or corn; pencils can be stuck into ends for holders.
- lace bells with yarn and beads for bands worn around the wrists or ankles.
- rubber bands stretched across a box to make a stringed instrument.
- rubber bands wrapped around an embroidery hoop; place the top hoop over the bands to hold them in place to make a small string instrument.
- sandpaper wrapped around blocks of wood to make scratch boards.
- bells glued or tied to tongue depressors for bell shakers.

Decorate each instrument with markers or puffy paints.

Specific Skills
- creative thinking
- patterns
- rhythm
- listening skills
- following directions
- problem solving

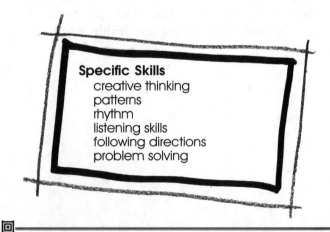

Easel Experiences

Use a variety of materials at the easel. Try such things as:

🔲 painting with evergreen branches

🔲 dipping chalk in saltwater before drawing

🔲 using two mediums, such as paint and crayons

🔲 cutting paper long and thin, square, round, triangular

🔲 using crayon chunks made of old crayon pieces melted in tins

🔲 using fingerpaint at the easel with sponge "brushes"

🔲 using colored chalk on dark papers

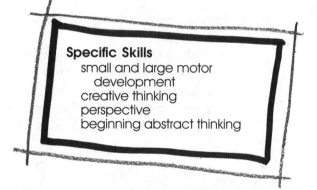

Specific Skills
small and large motor development
creative thinking
perspective
beginning abstract thinking

SUGGESTED MATERIALS

🔲 two tables of differing size

🔲 at least one easel

🔲 a large shelf for supplies

🔲 a small shelf or cart for materials specific to a project

🔲 a hanging rack or shelf for laying work to dry

🔲 close proximity to a sink, if at all possible

🔲 scrap boxes for paper, material, fake fur, plastic-type materials

🔲 hole punches: office type and the new cute shapes are nice

🔲 markers, crayons, colored pencils, chalk, paint, finger paint, payons (paint crayons)

🔲 newsprint, drawing paper, fingerpaint paper, construction paper, tissue paper, wrapping paper, wallpaper

🔲 sponge shapes and small sponges on clothespins for painting

🔲 paintbrushes of all sizes

🔲 lots of miscellaneous junk: buttons, rickrack, ribbon, feathers, cotton balls, confetti shapes, glitter

🔲 butcher paper to cover tables

🔲 wall space for hanging finished products

🔲 empty cans and plastic containers for holding small objects for projects

🔲 yarn of various colors and thicknesses

🔲 glue, colored glue, glue sticks, tape, colored tape, paste

🔲 glue brushes, Q-tips for fine work

🔲 moist clay, playdough, self-hardening clay

🔲 plastic mats for working with messy materials

🔲 eyedroppers

🔲 tongue depressors and popsicle sticks

🔲 paper towels

Multiple-Stage Art Activities

Create art experiences that go along with your thematic units and utilize a variety of materials. These can be created in two separate stages; as the first step dries, the second step is completed on another day, or in another area. For example:

1. Paint paper one day with a thin blue paint wash.
2. Add cotton ball clouds to create pictures during a weather unit.

Multiple-stage activities don't have to be confined to one center. Here, a student paints a picture of a garden at the easel.

1. Paint paper with watercolors of all colors.
2. Add shapes cut from wallpaper scraps to complete a picture of animals living in a rain forest. Try to create a camouflage effect with the paint and wallpaper.

1. Paint paper with watered-down glue, then lay tissue paper scraps of all colors all over the paper.
2. Later color a picture with black crayons. This might be used in a unit about the solar system, colors, or nutrition (draw fruits and veggies).

Later, he adds a story to his picture in the writing center.

Mosaics

There is more to making mosaics than just filling in space. I like the process that goes along with creating interesting mosaics, as well as the foolproof nature of the finished product. Young children can be creative with the materials they use to create texture and color, so that each one is different. But the basic shape that you gave them remains the same. It is controlled creativity.

With very young children, I precut the shapes from paper or tagboard. Then I allow them to fill in the space with materials. Their first project, very often a pumpkin, is simply filled in with paper scraps. This gets their fine muscles working, for I make them tear construction paper (cut into about 5" x 7" pieces) into a pile of scraps about the size of a thumb print. Once their paper is torn, they put glue onto the mosaic shape and rub it in with *one* finger. They then begin to fill the space with the torn paper scraps, repeating the process of rubbing in glue and adding paper scraps again and again until the shape is completely filled. The torn paper gives the shape texture, and the children see how important it is to fill the entire space with the materials. I have found that this is easier to understand when using only one medium to cover the shape. With a good group, I also encourage them to add facial features with black construction paper to create a jack-o-lantern face.

After this initial mosaic art experience, I move on to try different kinds of papers, cloth scraps, fake fur, seeds, yarn, aluminum foil, glitter, tiny beads, cornmeal, coffee grounds, styrofoam packing, sponge pieces, and just any old junk that has been donated and looks and feels interesting. I usually include a mosaic project in each of my thematic units. Some ideas that you might like to try include:

- a giant dinosaur covered with pieces of fake leather, vinyl, or styrofoam pieces.
- food items of their choice to place onto a giant cornucopia on a bulletin board during a unit on good nutrition.
- snowmen to use in retellings of favorite wintery snow stories.

- giant hearts filled with any type of materials.
- a mural of space with astronauts and/or spaceships made in mosaic form to give interest and texture to the picture. Aluminum foil and foil papers work well.
- flowers, using different materials for the petals and the greens. For example, the stem and leaves might be covered in green torn paper, while the petals are made up of bright cloth scraps, crumpled tissue paper, or a variety of seeds.

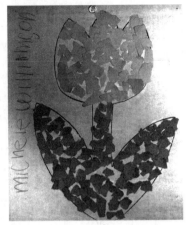

- animals: birds, reptiles, fish, mammals, etc. This is where their development in art expression is realized! Use a variety of materials on each animal, such as paper scraps and yarn, fuzzy wool scraps and feathers, fake leathers and string, or fake furs and leathers.

Older children can cut their own shapes, but I prefer to concentrate my younger children's efforts on their ability to think creatively about the materials they choose and filling the entire space with texture and color.

Tissue paper mosaics are an interesting way to discover color mixing and blending. The pieces can be piled on top of one another to get a variety of colors and blends. Spots can be added by putting on "dots" from hole punches. It's also fun to add details with a black marker over tissue paper mosaics.

Specific Skills
creative thinking
creative expression
fine motor development
abstract thinking and
   visualization
completing tasks
decision making

THE RESEARCH CENTER

Learning to research and report on information important to you uses a variety of domains. The type of research project I suggest is more than the typical effort of reading, writing about it, and handing it in.

My research center is designed around the *Self-Starter Kit for Independent Study*, by Edith Doherty and Louise Evans. In this program, each child designs his own specific project, investigating a very specific concept dealing with the thematic unit your class is currently studying. The kit explains the process in great detail, but I have adapted it for my own use.

You need to teach the process first, just as anything else. It might be wise to start with a class research project, to model the steps that individual children or small groups of children will complete as they design a project for their own use. The groups can work through individualized questions about one topic as you guide them through the first part of the process. The investigation can then be completed in cooperative groups, planning and completing a final, creative assignment to culminate the study.

1. First, a child chooses a topic to investigate in greater detail. For example, during a unit on tropical rain forests, a student wishes to learn more about three-toed sloths. Help him discover what he already knows about the animal: Why does he find it interesting enough to study in more detail? What kinds of things is he interested in learning about it? These will be his primary objectives.

2. When the child knows what he wishes to study, conference with him to make certain he has listed what he knows and

Name: __Beth Ingraham__   Date: __Oct. 12__

Fact Sheet for Independent Study: __Bats__

	Resource #1 Zipping, Zapping, Zooming Bats	Resource #2 C.D. Rom - Compton's Encycl.	Resource #3 Stellaluna
Question #1 What do bats eat?	mosquitoes gray bat - 3000 insects in 1 night moths, beetles, grasshoppers	brown bat - insects also fruit, flowers, sm. animals	fruit
Question #2 Are bats like birds?	long arm bones extra long finger bones like webbed hands "pups"- nurse (milk)	No - bats are mammals Have hooks on wings	No! nocturnal don't land on feet hang upside down
Question #3 Are there really bats that suck blood?	Vampire Bats - only kind Usually from cows	Central & S. America Vampire Bats	_____
Question #4 How do bats hang upside down?	by hooked claws on hands & toes	_____	hooks catch on branches
Question #5 How do they fly safely in the dark?	"echolocation" bouncing sound waves	high-pitched cries send sound waves reflected off obj. Ears are sensitive - react to waves	Use eyes to see - (?!) ✓ fact

Fig. 8-1

SUGGESTED MATERIALS

- a variety of papers
- writing tools
- a children's encyclopedia
- computer with a printer and CD-ROM (with encyclopedia)
- a variety of science textbooks
- nonfiction books dealing with concepts within the thematic unit
- trade books that teach information in the context of the story
- a selection of children's magazines such as *Ranger Rick, World,* and *Highlights for Children* that contain science articles related to your thematic unit
- models available that deal with the theme (such as earth-moon-sun or models of the human body
- charts and posters dealing with the theme
- library books, tapes, and recordings
- a variety of maps, atlases, and globes
- charts listing *Bloom's Taxonomy* verbs and steps in completing a research project, refined to meet the needs of your students (see page 147)

what he would like to learn. During the conference, help the student decide how much time he wishes to spend on this research project. The length of time the research will last will help determine how detailed the project can be. The student needs to plan how long he will spend investigating the material, then how much time will be spent creating a completed project.

3. Next, the student must find adequate resources for the investigation. Your school librarian can help, when she has available time, by assisting students in small groups. You can also supply your research center with many materials the students can use in the classroom.

4. Once the child has found ample resources, he may begin the research. I've given you a form (see Fig. 8-1; reproducible on page 192) that helps children learn how to take notes from multiple resources without simply copying sentences from each book. Because of the small space provided for each question, the child is limited to putting words and phrases in each box; he can then review his notes from all his resources together to answer each question.

As I said previously, independent research is probably best left for older children, but kindergartners and first graders can be guided through the research process and learn valuable skills while exploring topics of their own choosing.

5. Once all the research is completed, final objectives can be made for the project. First, the child chooses two to four objectives that require higher-level thinking strategies. He forms these by using a list of verbs that correspond to the levels of *Bloom's Taxonomy*. You can make a chart similar to the one on page 147 to assist the students in forming questions.

For example, students may be required to write two objectives, one using a verb from the first three levels, and one using a verb from the second three. In this way, you are requiring each child to research the subject he chooses, write objectives that require higher-level thinking skills, and then plan a project that will address his objectives. This allows you to individualize instruction for each child in your class without designing a different curriculum for each child. The children are creating their own curriculum; you are providing the scaffolding they need in order to complete this task.

6. Once the child has written his objectives, he should schedule a conference with you to plan his culminating project. The objectives he has written will direct his reporting about the information he has learned, but the final project will enable him to share this information with the class. The child should plan to do or make something that will demonstrate what he has learned.

It might be helpful in this stage to consider the seven intelligences.

For example, consider the possible investigations chosen by different students during the unit on the rain forest:

• A child who researches the three-toed sloth creates a diorama of a rain forest with a sloth in a tree. He places cards around the scene explaining the environment the sloth lives in. This child does not enjoy speaking in front of the class. He is free to choose a display with his written report.

• A child who researches children's books written about the rain forest writes a book of her own, and records it on audiotape. Her book, along with a selection of books she found in her research, are displayed in the reading center for others to enjoy.

• A child who researches endangered rain forest animals writes a song about them, and teaches it to the class. His report, along with the words and music to his song, is placed in the science center with a small electric keyboard so the students can learn to play the song.

Remember that each child should be given an opportunity to share his/her knowledge in the most appropriate way for that child. After this is accomplished, it is important to schedule a short evaluation conference in order to encourage each child to reflect on her learning, and the process she went through in her research. She might set goals for improving the experience or modifying the culminating project for her next individual investigation.

No activities need to be suggested, other than the description of the projects listed above, for each child designs his own research.

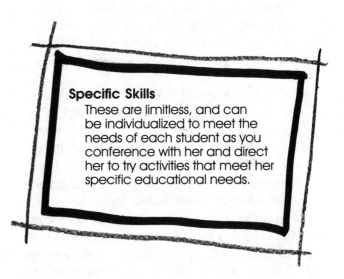

Specific Skills
These are limitless, and can be individualized to meet the needs of each student as you conference with her and direct her to try activities that meet her specific educational needs.

Words to Use to Plan Research Projects

Knowledge: list   identify   define   match   state

Comprehension: explain   locate   report   convert   paraphrase

Application: predict   relate   change   graph   plan

Analysis: web   infer   discover   analyze   distinguish

Synthesis: create   rewrite   design   rearrange   compose

Evaluation: select   criticize   judge   appraise   compare

THE COOKING CENTER

Another idea you might like to consider is a cooking center. I have seen this operate in a first grade classroom, and the children worked independently, following step-by-step instructions on task cards made by the teacher.

The recipes were simple and designed for one or two people. This classroom had an assistant whose job was to see that the food needed each day was put out just before center time, and put back in the refrigerator immediately after center time. She also monitored the center closely when any recipe called for the use of hot electrical equipment. You will have to judge your own situation to know if this would be a possibility for your classroom.

I operate a temporary cooking center in my kindergarten classrooms. I open the center one day each week, and I stay in that center if hot electrical appliances are used. I teach the children how to follow the recipe at the beginning of center time, and then call them over in small groups. In this way, every child visits this center in the one day it is open each week. This has worked well for me with very young children.

Obviously, this center takes some costly equipment, not to mention food throughout the year. There are many ways of funding a cooking center. One option is to include food as a consumable item, and assess a fee to parents at the beginning of the year. (In some states, parents can be charged annually for consumable materials.) Another way is to have parents volunteer to bring in specific food items, such as flour, milk, margarine, etc.

You can also have parents sign up for specific projects. In this case, you would post a list of the cooking projects you plan to have during the year during an open house or conference day. Ask each parent to sign up for one project. Then, a week before the project, send home a note explaining what ingredients the parents will need to send in with their child. I have seen this work very well.

Still another way is to ask your parent group to sponsor your cooking center, purchasing equipment and food as needed throughout the year. I have found this to be the easiest method. Some parent groups will open an account with a local grocer for you, while others will ask that you purchase the food first, then turn in receipts to be reimbursed. Either way, it is efficient and a nice way for the parent organization to feel it is spending its money in ways that will benefit each child.

Don't forget to ask if grant money is available. Some states offer grants for food and cooking equipment in connection with nutrition education programs. This works very nicely for an entire elementary building, a grade level, or just one classroom.

Gooey Grahams

1 graham cracker

1 scoop of peanut butter

Spread gooey peanut butter over graham cracker.

Look	Smell
Listen	and
Touch	Taste

Suggested Activities

◙ Cook authentic multicultural foods while studying another country.

◙ Cook for your thematic unit.

◙ Bake for an Author's Tea or Parent Open House.

◙ Cook for every letter of the alphabet.

◙ Cook food items to go with a particular book you are reading. For example, make some muffins with plum jam when reading *Thy Friend, Obadiah*.

Specific Skills
vocabulary
comprehension
following directions
measurement
sequential order
equivalency
addition
fractions
five senses
changes in matter
temperature
fine and gross motor
   development

SUGGESTED MATERIALS

◙ a storage cart for equipment and food

◙ a small refrigerator or the use of a refrigerator and freezer

◙ a small oven or large toaster oven

◙ a burner or stove

◙ an electric skillet

◙ a waffle iron

◙ a popcorn popper, preferably with a plastic dome lid (see-through)

◙ glass cookware (so children can see what happens without putting their noses in the pan)

◙ baking pans and muffin tins (small muffin cup size)

◙ hand mixer

◙ plastic containers for storing food

◙ knives, forks, and spoons

◙ hot pads and towels, sponges

◙ spatulas, large spoons, whisk, grater, potato peeler, etc.

◙ measuring spoons and cups (several sets)

◙ colander, mixing bowls in a variety of sizes

◙ small pitchers

◘ Chapter 8 ◘

Resources

Albyn, Carole Lisa, and Webb, Lois Sinaiko. *The Multicultural Cookbook for Students*. Phoenix, AR: The Oryx Press, 1993.

Blakey, Nancy. *The Mudpies Activity Book: Recipes for Invention*. Berkeley, CA: Ten Speed Press, 1989.

Diehn, Gwen, and Krautwurst, Terry. *Nature Crafts for Kids*. Asheville, NC: Altamont Press, 1992.

Doherty, Edith, and Evans, Louise. *Self-Starter Kit for Independent Study*. East Windsor Hill, CT: Synergetics, 1980.

Englebaugh, Debi. *Art Through Children's Literature*. (Creative Art Lessons for Caldecott Books) Englewood, CO: Teacher Ideas Press, 1994.

Gomez, Aurelia. *Crafts of Many Cultures*. New York: Scholastic, 1992.

Kruise, Carol Sue. *Those Bloomin' Books*. Littleton, CO: Libraries Unlimited, 1987.

Terzian, Alexandra M. *The Kids' Multicultural Art Book*. Charlotte, VT: Williamson Publishing, 1993.

Veitch, Beverly, and Harms, Thelma. *Cook and Learn: Pictorial Single Portion Recipes*. Menlo Park, CA: Addison-Wesley, 1981.

Chapter 9

Physical and Social/Emotional Development Centers

Underneath the knocker there was a notice which said:

> *PLES RING IF AN RNSER
> IS REQIRD.*

Underneath the bell-pull there was a notice which said:

> *PLEZ CNOKE IF AN RNSR
> IS NOT REQID.*

These notices had been written by Christopher Robin, who was the only one in the forest who could spell.

> — A. A. Milne,
> *Winnie-the-Pooh*

 oung children learn through play. Centers designed around play invite the children to use reasoning skills, problem-solving strategies, abstract thinking, cooperative learning strategies, and oral language with their peers. Physical and social/emotional development centers are too often absent from primary classrooms. The gap between kindergarten and first grade is seen most clearly in these areas.

The most effective kindergarten teachers have learned how to use these areas to meet objectives across the curriculum. Primary teachers might gain many ideas by visiting a good kindergarten classroom and observing these centers. Imagine the cognitive learning that can take place in these areas when the environment is designed for the appropriate age level, organized within the framework of each thematic unit. Be careful to remember that the work must be meaningful and purposeful for the child, and in the case of these centers, the work must come naturally from the activity of the area.

For example, when learning about food and nutrition, it would be a natural extension of the child's learning to place a restaurant in the role play area. The work placed within that environment should involve the children in actions they would go through if they were working in or eating at a restaurant: reading a menu, writing down an order for food, reading a recipe in order to prepare the food, following the written directions (and comprehending them) of a recipe, trying out foods from a specific culture when the restaurant is based on another country, adding the cost of the meal, giving change after payment. These activities teach valuable lessons without detracting from the natural play of the child.

Including food pyramid worksheets or math papers asking the child to answer story problems about giving change, or having the children write reports about France because they have chosen to make this a French restaurant, are not activities that are part of the play of the area. They detract from the activity that the children would naturally become engaged in within this area.

Imagine the environment that you and your class have designed, then focus on objectives in your curriculum that might be learned as the children play in this environment. This will help you come up with authentic play experiences that also teach your students lessons you must make certain to expose them to. And, of course, don't forget to ask your students for ideas! They come up with quality, authentic, age-appropriate environments.

The same idea holds true in the gross motor area. During the unit on foods and nutrition, set up a small exercise course and have the children learn a variety of exercises that they can do daily to stay physically fit. Ask them to put an aerobics routine together for the class to learn. During a unit on space, ask your students to build a spaceship or command post. Once it is built, they might place necessary signs and directions within the area. Before taking it down, they can draw the unit to see if someone else can rebuild it

another day. The lessons are there to be learned surrounded by true play experiences important to the emotional, social, and physical development of the child.

Gross Motor Center

The gross motor area in my classroom is primarily a block center; however, the activities here change occasionally. Bean bags, the balance beam, ring toss, and exercises come and go through this center location. The area also contains small blocks, trains, and cars.

Interactive charts about transportation, block building, and machines come and go. Paper and pencils are needed as children create signs that are a necessary part of the construction they are working on. A lot of cooperative skills are learned here as well, as the children decide together what will be built, how the blocks will be placed, and how they will be put away.

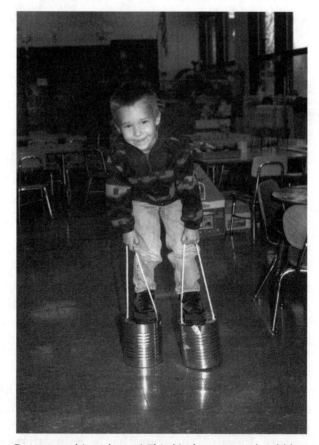

Do not try this at home! This kindergartner should be using these stilts in the carpeted block area rather than on slippery tile, but he couldn't miss a good photo opportunity.

My block shelf is very organized. The block shapes are traced onto construction paper, and attached to the block shelf with clear plastic contact paper. The children must put the blocks back where they belong after each session.

The children I taught during my student teaching in a multiage second-third combination created extraordinary and massive structures in their block area. There is no doubt in my mind that at least one architect was nurtured in that classroom. They re-created smaller versions of their large block buildings with Legos™, and drew detailed pictures of the structures they created. The abstract thinking that developed before my eyes was astounding.

Extensive and complicated buildings can be left out for days, allowing several children to add and modify structures. So much is gained by young children as they work in these environments, it is a shame to move them out of the classroom so early.

Making and Using Recycled Games in the Gross Motor Area

During a thematic unit on the environment, my class decided to create some games out of recycled or reused materials. They didn't have the play equipment that they wanted, and I thought it would be nice for these children to discover that games could be created out of materials they have around their own houses instead of feeling as though they had to have ready-made games. Because so many children cannot afford much in the way of material for gross motor activities, this was a good lesson in how to create fun things to do instead of watching television.

We talked about the games they would like most to play, and listed them on a large chart. Then we thought of how these games were made, and what would be needed to create them ourselves. We found pictures of them in old catalogs and toys store ads. The children discussed what they liked most about each game. Then I began collecting materials. We made the following items together, after

I had brought in most of the materials. The children helped collect pea gravel from the playground and assisted in putting the games together. While I led them in their creation, they gave input into how we went about making the games. They took an active role in the design and the assembly of each activity. Although they didn't actually design each item, they were involved enough to think they did. Here is what we made and liked the best.

1. Bowling

We took old plastic juice bottles with lids and filled them half full of pea gravel. Then we found an old baseball and a toy bowling ball in a closet filled with used and/or lost playground equipment. We made up different games to play similar to bowling.

2. Stilts

Large empty coffee cans became stilts when we punched two holes in the sides of the bottom of the can, straight across from each other and close to the rim. Then we took a sturdy cotton rope and put it through the holes, so that it looped under the "lid" and through the holes. I tied the ends inside the can. The length of rope depends upon the height of your children, but should be long enough for them to hold on to as they walk on the cans. Making it a bit shorter than they need to stand up straight helps them remember to pull on the ropes as they walk, so that they do not walk off without the can held to their feet! This was the favorite recycled toy by a large margin!

3. Ball Toss

We cut the bottom out of old gallon milk jugs and used them to toss and catch a lightweight rubber ball. An old yarn ball or tennis ball works well for this, too. My students enjoyed using a variety of balls in this game, as they found that their technique had to change with the weight of the ball they were tossing.

4. Drop in the Can

We collected old wooden one-inch cubes that were lost from sets of manipulatives in our classroom. Most of these were so old that the paint had worn off. Then we took several old cans and covered them with decorated paper. We stood over the cans, using the largest first, and simply dropped the cubes into the cans. We kept track of how many we were able to get into the cans for each size. The children were surprised how much more difficult the task became when the can got smaller.

We also created a similar game with bean bags and a large coffee can. Instead of dropping the bean bags in, the children had to toss them into the can. The degree of difficulty changed by moving back two steps every time you put a bean bag into the can.

Working in the role play center is serious business.

The Role Play Center

The role play center changes on a regular basis. It begins as a house, but changes to such things as a grocery store, doctor's office, post office, pet shop, business office, music shop, toy workshop, bakery, restaurant, or publishing company. At the beginning of the year, I plan the areas, but once the children have learned how to work in these settings, I let them dictate what will develop in the area, planned around the thematic units.

Appropriate literacy activities are built into the dramatic play. Message pads, grocery lists, medical charts, checks and money, appointment books, letters and envelopes, menus, telephone and address books, magazines, and recipes are used to give the children realistic purposes for using literacy skills. This motivates them to take risks in their development of literacy skills. I have seen this interest trans-fer over into the literacy centers, as my students worked at writing and reading tasks in order to use these skills in the role play center.

The children utilize dress-ups and props in the role play center to practice the skills they need to go about their day in a grown-up world. Before opening a new area, we brainstorm together what items will be needed. After all the items are collected, I model behavior that is appropriate in the area. I often allow the children to help with this. I ask for volunteers to come into the center as I explain the materials and tasks that are there. Each child who volunteers shows the group what someone in this place would be doing in a real-life situation.

For example, if the center is set up as a doctor's office, I might ask the children who would be present in this place. The child who offers "a receptionist" would come into the center with me and model what a receptionist does in a doctor's office. Once this is accomplished, I also ask the class if there is anything else the receptionist would do, in order to get several ideas and all the children involved. We would then think of someone else who would be present here: for instance, the nurse, the doctor, parents, and children.

With each new person, we go through the activity each would be involved in at this area. The children see the idea that each person has a role to play and a purpose for being in the location, and they go about the work they do there with much thoughtfulness.

When I do this before each new center is opened, the behavior remains on-task and purposeful work is accomplished. I see children experimenting with literacy in real-life situations, rather than becoming overly silly because they are playing the part of a make-believe person.

If you are a teacher of children older than kindergartners, I would encourage you not to overlook these two centers. Much can be learned here, whether the children are five or eight or ten. Puppetry, creative dramatics, reader's theater, and storytelling can easily be developed with older students within the boundaries of a creative drama or role play center. Some of the favorite ideas other teachers have shared with me are:

1. A Take-Apart Center: Old electrical appliances and tools are placed in a center for the children to take apart and examine. Caution: Cut cords first.

2. A Real Estate Office: The children draw pictures of the houses they are selling, write ads and brochures, price the homes, and sell them to children in other classrooms.

3. A Pet Store: After visiting a veterinarian, a class borrows a pet or two. The children take care of the animals along with some stuffed animals they bring in. (Class pets that are usually in the science center may be used rather than asking a local pet store for some.)

In a kindergarten classroom, the children can price pets for ten cents each or less, and use pennies, nickels, and dimes to "sell" them and give change. Early elementary children might write ads for the animals, displaying them around the school.

THE GROSS MOTOR/ BLOCK CENTER

Develop a Balance Beam Activity

Make a giant die with pictures of a human body: hands on head, hands on hips, holding a scarf, walking backward, etc. Put the die out when the balance beam is up, and the children will walk on the beam according to what is thrown on the die.

Create a Zoo

Place plastic animals in the center during an appropriate thematic unit. Have the children create a zoo, including signs, a map, and areas that resemble the animals' natural habitats.

Specific Skills
cooperation
large motor development
following directions

Specific Skills
vocabulary
oral language development
large and small motor development
abstract thinking
creative thinking
problem solving
cooperation

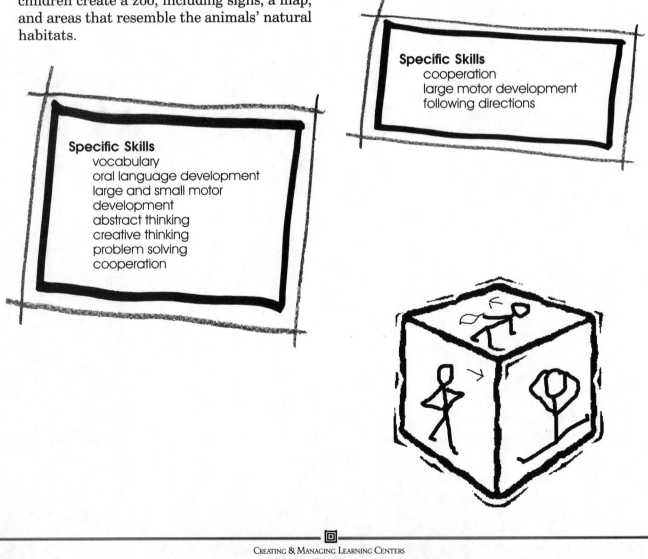

Create Architectural Models

Hang pictures of statues or architecturally unique buildings in the block area. Have the children create models of the ones they like the most.

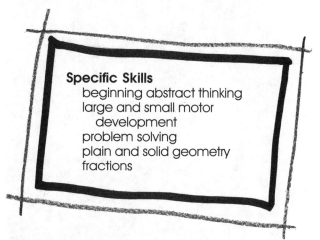

Specific Skills
- beginning abstract thinking
- large and small motor development
- problem solving
- plain and solid geometry
- fractions

Use and Create Machines

Place simple machines in the block center. Have the children experience using them to move blocks for building. Create new inventions using several simple machines.

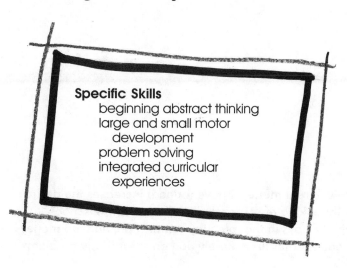

Specific Skills
- beginning abstract thinking
- large and small motor development
- problem solving
- integrated curricular experiences

SUGGESTED MATERIALS

- block shelf with patterns of block shapes on shelves
- wooden blocks (plain and colored set)
- cars, trucks, trains
- boards to use as planks
- pulleys, levers, and other simple machines
- road signs
- materials for creating signs needed in constructions
- books and charts dealing with block building and transportation
- shelf space or basket for books
- chart stand for interactive charts and transportation songs
- old recycled telephone (wall phone is nice) for calling repair shops
- Legos™ (in a variety of sizes)
- balance beam
- exercise mats
- ring toss, bean bags, gross motor games
- small jogging trampoline

THE
ROLE PLAY/
DRAMATIC CENTER

Create a Pet Shop

Create a pet shop with one stuffed animal brought in by each child. The children price their "pets" and use play money to make purchases. Or, real* money could be used to give practice in making change.

Have children use order forms and telephone message pads, and write advertisements to sell the pets. Place books about the care and feeding of the animals in the center.

Specific Skills
oral language development
cooperation
literacy skills designed
    around tasks (according
    to age level)
money and making change

---

* When using money in a role play center, I like to use real money. I have found it increases the desire to be correct when counting change, and adds to the taking of responsibility. Except for the school supply store, the sales are still pretend and the money stays in the role play center. I provide the money, and it is counted and accounted for at the end of each center time. Rarely do I encounter any problems with money disappearing.

Open a Grocery Store

Set up a grocery store with food items (empty containers) brought in by the children. Organize the shelves according to the five food groups, and after shopping, the shopper becomes the stock person and must put the groceries back according to their nutritional value. Literacy materials can include grocery lists, order lists for the grocer, advertisements, and displays. Food samples may be created by students designing special sandwiches or treats.

Specific Skills
nutrition
classification
literacy and math skills
    according to the tasks
    assigned for your level
vocabulary
oral language development
cooperation

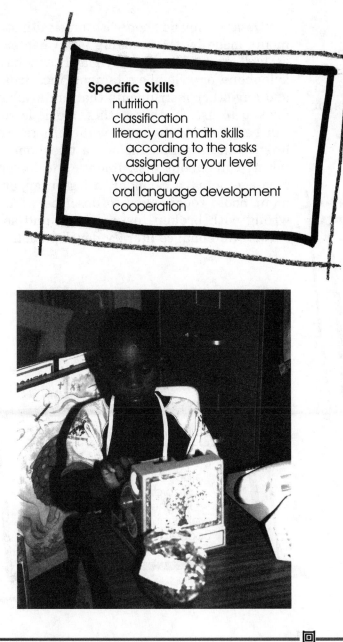

- housekeeping furniture: small table and chairs, wooden kitchen set, baby bed, small rocker, high chair
- old, recycled telephone
- an old bathroom scale
- suitcase and clothes for practice in folding and putting away
- small plastic hangers for practice in putting clothes away
- small grocery carts and/or baby stroller
- small tub or water table for washing a plastic baby
- literacy materials specific to each environment created
- dress-ups and props for each environment
- puppets and puppet stage
- musical instruments, simple songs to play on charts
- charts appropriate for display during each new area

Create a Publishing Company

Create a publishing company, where the students can bring their books to be published. An editor will need to approve all books before printing. Sales and promotion of the books will need to be designed. Interviews with authors should be scheduled with other classrooms. Books will have to be priced and inventory must be accounted for if books will actually be copied and sold.

This might also be set up as a newspaper office, with the students actually preparing a newspaper on a regular basis and selling it in the cafeteria. Money could be used to pay for duplicating costs, or to purchase new books for the classroom.

Specific Skills
 literacy and math skills
  according to the tasks
  assigned to your level
 recordkeeping
 money and making change
 oral language development
 creative problem solving
 higher-level thinking strategies

Start a Music Store

Design a music shop with musical instruments made by the students (see Chapter 8) as well as an electric keyboard, autoharp, xylophone or xylopipes, tambourine, drums, and any other instruments that are available for you to use. In this setting, music lessons can be given by students, while others "fix" broken instruments. Include a telephone for taking calls about instruments and lessons. Message notes, a calendar, a lesson appointment book, repair slips to describe what is wrong with broken instruments, and song sheets will enhance literacy development.

Specific Skills
 problem solving
 creative thinking
 literacy and math skills
  according to the tasks
  designed for your level
 oral language development
 cooperation

Open a School Store

Create a school supply store, selling items such as notebook paper, pencils and pens, erasers, glue, and markers. Open the store before school starts in the morning, and allow children from other classrooms to purchase needed supplies. Students should keep track of the money taken in, keep accurate records, advertise store hours and/or sale items, etc.

Specific Skills
record keeping
money and making change
writing advertisements
problem solving
leadership and
responsibility skills

Run a Restaurant

Design a restaurant, complete with a menu of items the children can actually make. Display the recipes in the "kitchen," while the customers sit at tables in the restaurant. Food may be priced and sold for pretend or real money. This is one idea that could be used with any age group. The goals for the activities would differ according to the age of the children. This may be combined with a cooking center.

Specific Skills
cooperation
oral language development
following directions
comprehension skills
measurement
fractions
literacy and math skills
according to the tasks
assigned for your level

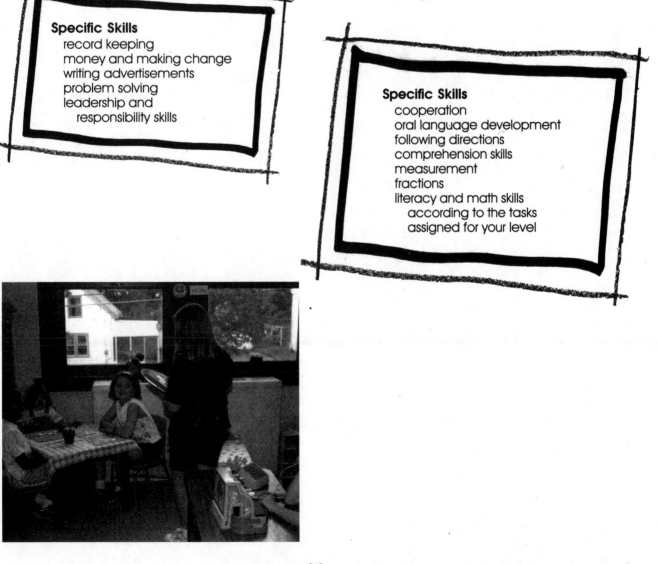

Appendix

Week of _____

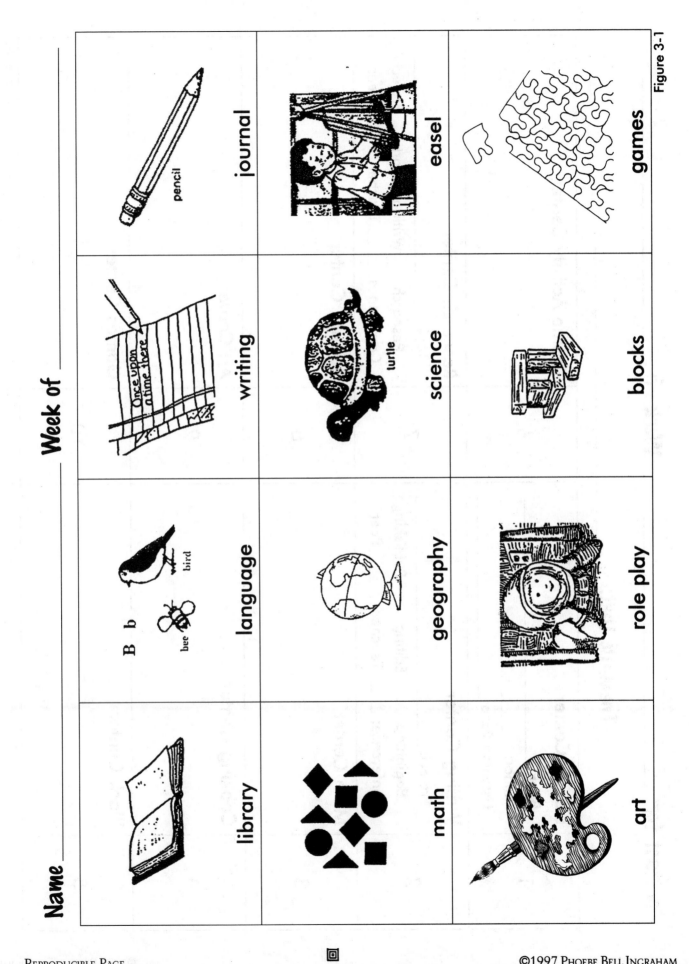

		journal pencil
		easel
		games
library	B b bird bee language	writing	journal pencil

Figure 3-1

Contract for: _____

Week of: _____

Thematic Unit: _____

1	**Library Center** Book: _____ Author: _____ Listening Tape: _____	6	**Theme Activity Center**
2	**Writing Center** Project: _____ Beginning Editing Publishing Conference: ___ Teacher ___ Peer	7	**Research Center** Topic: _____ Research Writing Report Project Conference: ___ Teacher ___ Peer
3	**Math Center**	8	**Science Center**
4	**Cooking Center**	9	**Art Center**
5	**Block Center**	10	**Games Center**

Figure 3-2

Contract for: _____

Week of: _____

Thematic Unit: _____

 B b bee bird	**Language Center**	 **Library Center**
	**Writing Center**	 **Role Play Center**
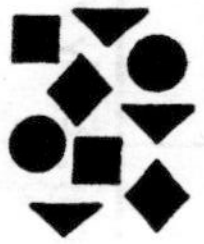	**Math Center**	 **Science Center** turtle
	**Geography Center**	 **Computer Lab**
	**Block Center**	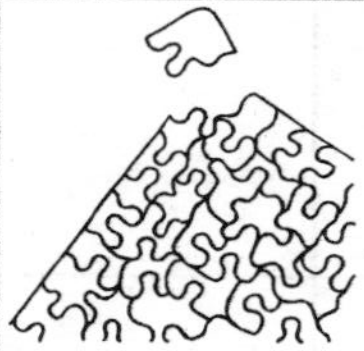 **Games Center**
	**Art Center**	 **Easel Center**

©1997 PHOEBE BELL INGRAHAM

Figure 3-3

Name_____ Month_____

Center	Week 1	Week 2	Week 3	Week 4	Week 5
Art 					
Language Arts  B b bee bird					
Reading 					
Computer 					
Math 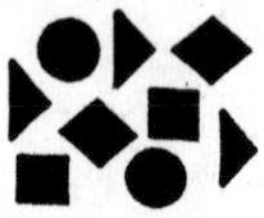					
Science  turtle					
Theme 					
Games 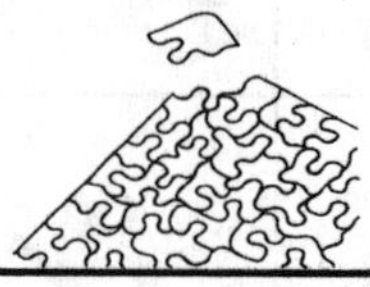					

Center Chart for Mrs. Carla Amburgey, Early Primary Teacher, Middletown, OH

Figure 3-4

Name: _____

Week of: _____

Language (B b / bird / bee)	* jobs	2 job	3 job	4 job
Math (shapes)	* job	2 job	3 job	4 job
Writing	* job	name	journal	
Science (turtle)	* job	2 job	3 job	2 books
Library	3 books	tape	job	job
Geography (globe)	* job	2 job	map	2 books
Role Play	* job	write	read	
Computers	words	sentences	game	
Art	* job — write	2 job — write		
Blocks	read	build	write	clean up
Easel	* job — write	2 job — write		
Games (puzzle)	1 game	2 game	3 game	puzzle

Figure 3-5

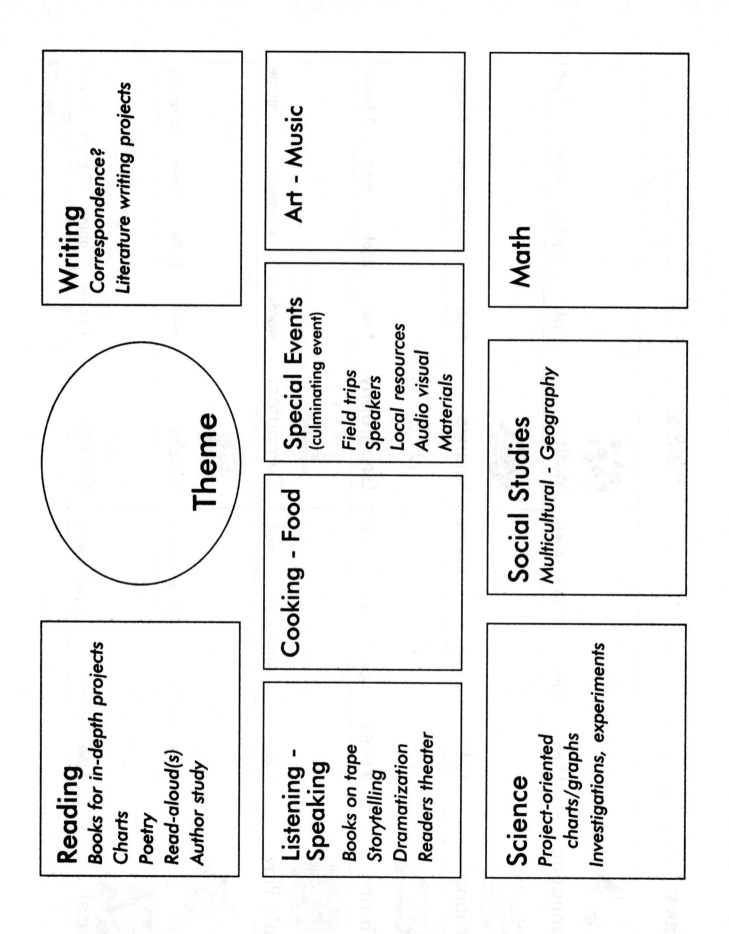

Writing
Correspondence?
Literature writing projects

Art - Music

Math

Theme

Special Events
(culminating event)
Field trips
Speakers
Local resources
Audio visual
Materials

Cooking - Food

Social Studies
Multicultural - Geography

Reading
Books for in-depth projects
Charts
Poetry
Read-aloud(s)
Author study

Listening - Speaking
Books on tape
Storytelling
Dramatization
Readers theater

Science
Project-oriented
charts/graphs
Investigations, experiments

Figure 4-5

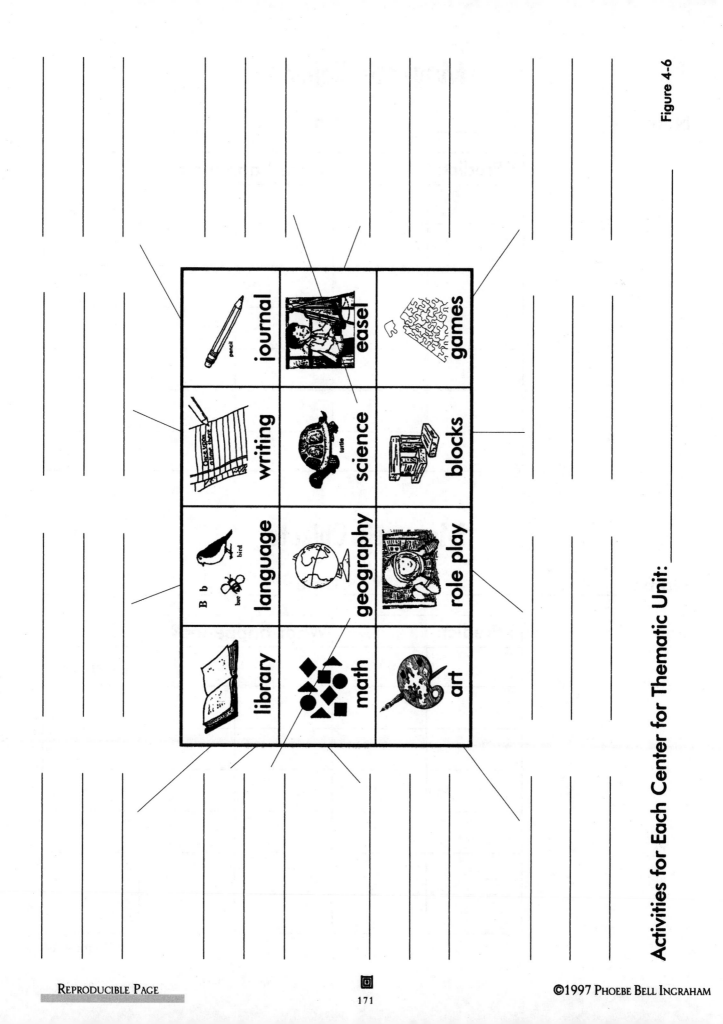

Activities for Each Center for Thematic Unit: _____

©1997 Phoebe Bell Ingraham

Figure 4-6

Magnetic Objects

Name:_____   Date:_____

I Predict:		What happened?		
				Correct?

Magnetic Objects

Name:_____   Date:_____

I Predict:		What happened?		
				Correct?

Figure 4-14

First Quarter Anecdotal Record

Name _____ Birthdate _____

Social / Emotional Development and Work Habits:

Physical Development:

Cognitive Development:

Figure 5-1

Anecdotal Notes:_____ Name_____

_____

Monday	Tuesday	Wednesday	Thursday	Friday

_____

Monday	Tuesday	Wednesday	Thursday	Friday

Figure 5-2

Monthly Journal Check

Name:_____

Month:	Sept.	Oct.	Nov.	Dec.	Jan.	Feb.	Mar.	Apr.	May
Precompositional I:									
Scribbles									
Mock letters									
A few letters or numbers									
A small string of letters or numbers									
Scribble drawings									
Precompositional II:									
Isolated letters (inv. spelling)									
Repeated groups of letters (letter strings)									
Incomplete alphabet or list of numerals									
One memorized or copied word									
Designs with letter writing									
Objects/beg. picture stories									
Precompositional III:									
List of two to ten words									
Mock words in a long list									
Very hard to read message (inv. spelling)									
Complete alphabet									
Word boundaries to separate words									
Copied phrase/message									
Object/pict. stories with inv. spellings									
Detailed picture stories (few or no letters)									
Compositional I:									
Simple message (I love you)									
List of 10 or more words									
Complete alphabet with over 10 words									
Rebus sentence (I like [picture])									
Picture story with inv. spellings (assoc.)									
Labeled objects with real words									
Compositional II:									
Original message (complete thought)									
Message of two or more sentences									
List of short sentences									
Short letter									
Print tells the message (picture less imp.)									
Compositional III:									
Long story with plot (4 or more sentences)									
Long letter that sticks to the subject									
Picture complements story									

Adapted from: Lamme/Green Scale of Children's Development, 1987

Figure 5-4

Math Jobs for _____

	1	2	3	4	5	6	7	8	9
pattern tasks									
classification									
number tasks									
choice jobs									

Math Jobs for _____

	1	2	3	4	5	6	7	8	9
pattern tasks									
classification									
number tasks									
choice jobs									

Figure 5-5

Autumn Leaves

Red and yellow, orange and brown,

Autumn leaves are falling down.

Whirling, twirling, see them fall.

I can count _____ leaves in all!

Reading Log

Name _____

Date	Title of the book	Tell me about the book	☺ ☹

Class Reading Log

Genre:_____

Date	Reader	Title of Book	Comments

Tell Me the Story

First,	Next,	Last,

Name _____

😊 I liked this story.　　😞 I did not like this story.

Name _____

My book is: _____

Draw about the beginning, middle and end of your book. Write about each picture.

Beginning	Middle	End

181

Words that Rhyme

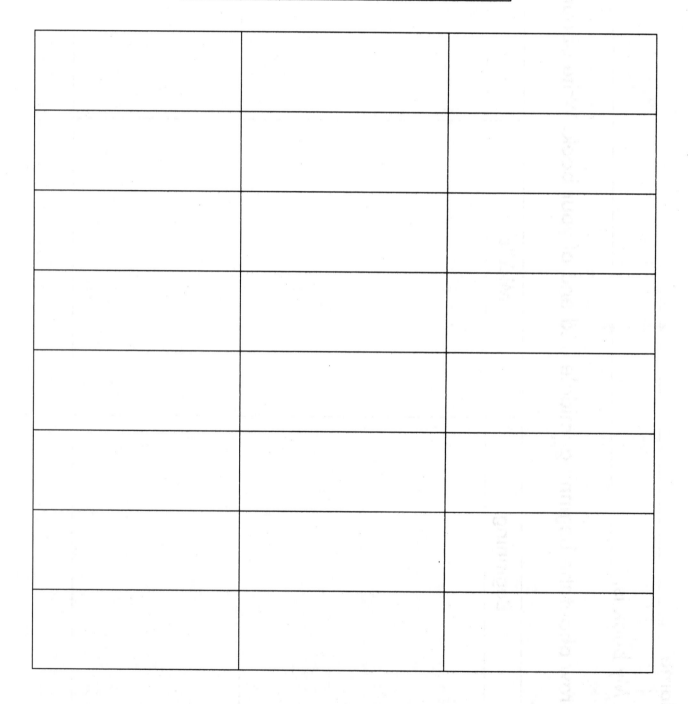

Thematic Unit: _____

Name: _____ **Date:** _____

[blank box for drawing]

New vocabulary words I can use:

1. _____ 2. _____ 3. _____

I discovered that _____

_____

_____

_____

My favorite activity was _____

_____

_____

_____

name _____

m & m® Graph

9						
8						
7						
6						
5						
4						
3						
2						
1						
	red m&m	green m&m	brown m&m	blue m&m	yellow m&m	orange m&m

How many red? _____   How many blue? _____

How many green? _____   How many yellow? _____

How many brown? _____   How many orange? _____

How many m & m's in all? _____

Rock Graph

Name _____

Rock	1	2	3	4	5	6
white						
gray						
black						
brown						
red						
two colors						
three colors						
four colors						
five colors						

Observation Sheet

Scientist: _____ Observation Date: _____

I looked under a:

_____ microscope
_____ hand lens
_____ bare eye

Draw what you observe:

Describe your observation in words:

_____

_____

_____

_____

_____

_____

Australia (copy to color)

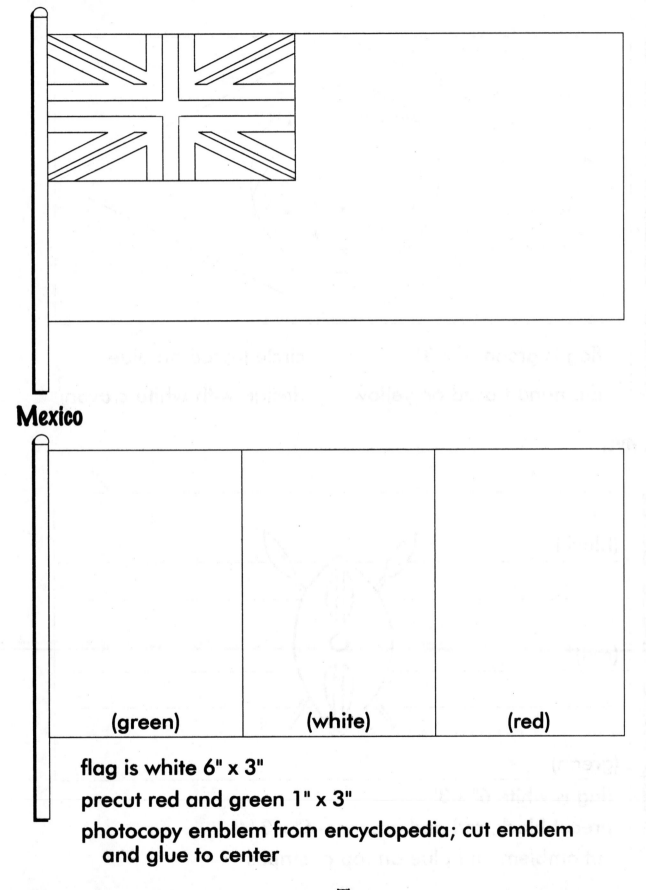

Mexico

(green)   (white)   (red)

flag is white 6" x 3"

precut red and green 1" x 3"

photocopy emblem from encyclopedia; cut emblem
and glue to center

Brazil

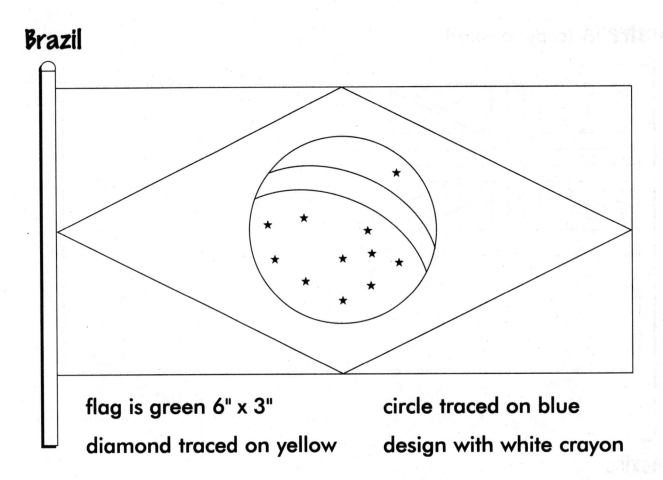

flag is green 6" x 3"   circle traced on blue

diamond traced on yellow   design with white crayon

Kenya

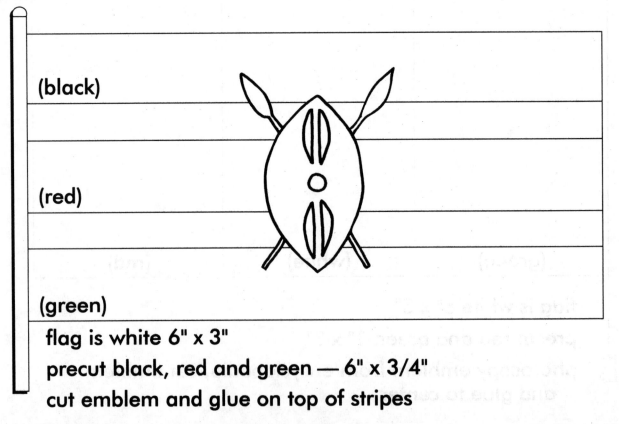

(black)

(red)

(green)

flag is white 6" x 3"

precut black, red and green — 6" x 3/4"

cut emblem and glue on top of stripes

Italy · France

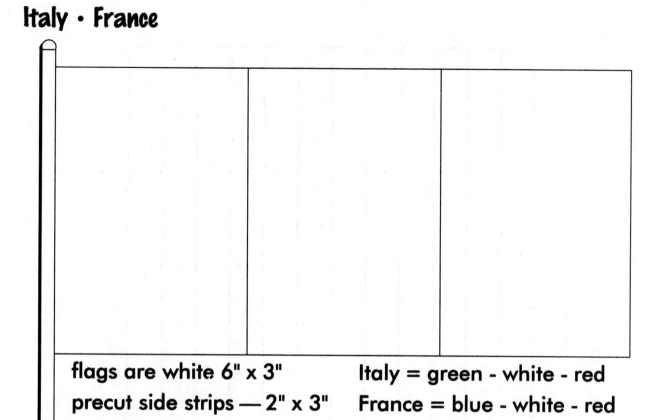

flags are white 6" x 3"

precut side strips — 2" x 3"

Italy = green - white - red

France = blue - white - red

People's Republic of China

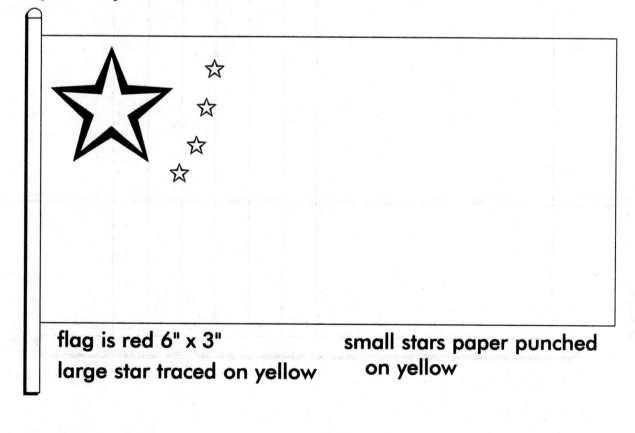

flag is red 6" x 3"

large star traced on yellow

small stars paper punched
on yellow

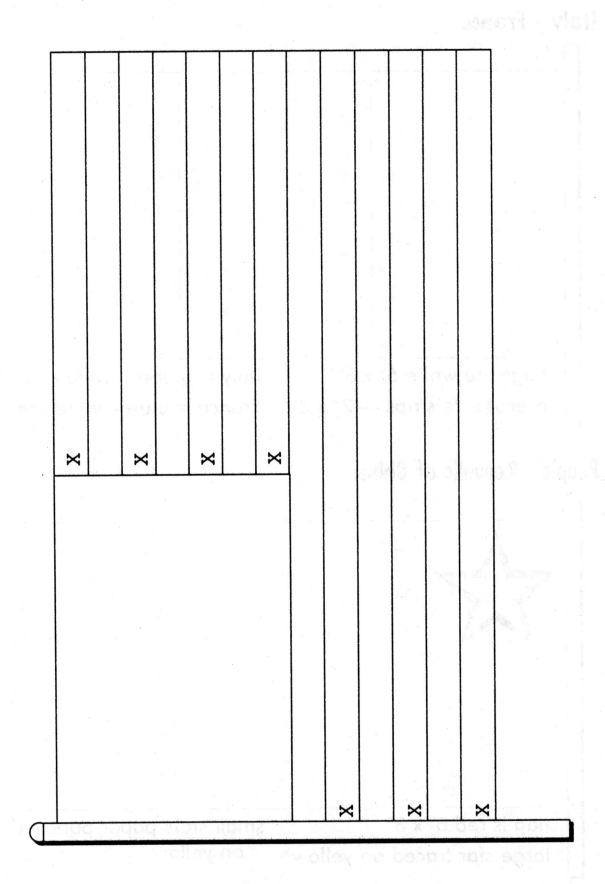

U.S.A.

Tangram

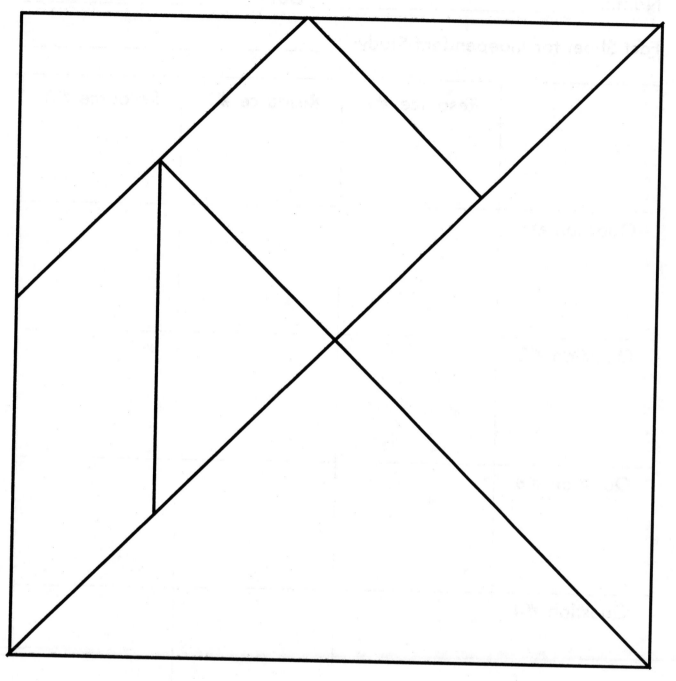

Name:_____ Date:_____

Fact Sheet for Independent Study: _____

	Resource #1	Resource #2	Resource #3
Question #1			
Question #2			
Question #3			
Question #4			
Question #5			

5150

326241

192

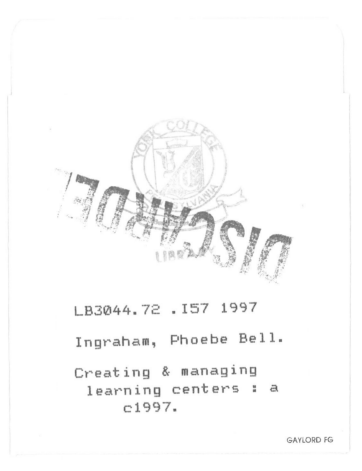